BREAKFAST
at the
VICTORY

Breakfast

at the

Victory

THE MYSTICISM
OF ORDINARY EXPERIENCE

James P. Carse

HarperSanFrancisco
A Division of HarperCollins*Publishers*

HarperSanFrancisco and the author, in association with the Rainforest Action Network, will facilitate the planting of two trees for every one tree used in the manufacture of this book.

FIRST EDITION

Text design by George Brown

Library of Congress Cataloging-in-Publication Data
Carse, James P.
Breakfast at the Victory : the mysticism of ordinary experience /
James P. Carse — 1st ed.
p.   cm.
ISBN 0–06–251170–x (cloth : alk. paper)
ISBN 0–06–251171–8 (pbk. : alk. paper)
1. Mysticism.   2. Spiritual life.   3. Psychology, Religious.
I. Title.
BL625.C34   1994
291.4'22—dc20   94–5010
                                                             CIP

94 95 96 97 98 ❖ RRD(H) 10 9 8 7 6 5 4 3 2 1

To the memory of
David Bradley Carse, 1934–1988,
and that last, perfect shot.

Preface

M AYBE you'll find my boots in Spain," Charles said.

Charles was dying of cancer. I had stopped in to see him on my way to Spain where I planned to walk the old pilgrimage route from the French border to Santiago de Compostela in the northwest corner of Spain. As I sat on the edge of his bed, I wondered whether I would ever see Charles again. He had a different question. He wanted to know my spiritual goals for this pilgrimage. I said I hoped I would learn the goals while on the journey. He wasn't satisfied with this. I tried to make the same point in a more complicated way. Then he interrupted me with the remark about his boots.

"They just gave out," he added. "So I put them on a stone wall by the road and limped on in my bare feet."

The comment had a clarifying abruptness. It was a reminder that pilgrimages are as much about sore feet as about souls. After finishing college in the early sixties, Charles spent several years in Europe as a penniless and unpublished poet. It was then that he took a long, solitary walk across Spain, "to look for the meaning of it All."

Finding nothing, he came home, married Juliet, a fellow exile poet, became a carpenter, and raised three sons.

Almost four weeks into the pilgrimage, I started up into the Cantabrian mountains, hoping to reach an inn in the small village of El Cebreiro before nightfall. Soaked by days of heavy rain and snow, the narrow farm road was ankle deep in mud and cow dung. The muck had seeped down into my shoes and I could feel new blisters forming. I was taking one step at a time, careful where I would place each foot, when I saw the outline of a familiar object crushed in the mire. Gently I tugged at the old boot until it came free. The sole was gone but its essential structure remained. So I propped it up on a stone wall to take several photographs of it. Later I sent one to Charles.

When I got home I went by to see Charles and found that Juliet had hung the photograph above his bed. He amused all his visitors with the story of the boots and how I found one that could have been his. As he told it, the folly of his youthful quest took on the echoes of a solemn medieval pilgrimage adding depth and color to his subsequent journey as husband, father, craftsman, friend. The certainty of his imminent death edged this brief tale with the unknown. His delight in telling it made us think there was something larger than death.

In this book I have lifted out similarly modest events from my own life journey and propped them up for closer inspection. They came and went without announcing they were special. I felt their resonance only later, in some cases, many years later. For that reason it is not important when they occur in the narrative of my life. It is important only that upon reflection, I can glimpse how they open onto the un-known.

All experience, to borrow an expression of the mystics, is bounded by the boundless. Every step on our journey adds to what we know but it also reveals there is no end to knowing. This book is an invitation to see how extraordinary the ordinary is when we rediscover it by way of the mystical.

BREAKFAST
at the
VICTORY

Breakfast at the Victory

In one of the great court banquets, everyone was seated according to rank, waiting the entry of the King. In came a plain,
shabby man and took a seat above everyone else. His boldness
angered the prime minister who ordered the newcomer to
identify himself. Was he a minister? No. More. Was he the
King? No. More. "Are you then God?" asked the prime minister. "I am above that also," replied the poor man. "There is
nothing beyond God," retorted the prime minister. "That
nothing," came the response, "is me."

A SUFI PARABLE

ERNIE CERTAINLY didn't leave the army with the intention of setting up a mystical luncheonette. I was a
regular at the place for a long time before I began to
see the mysticism in it myself.

For nearly thirty years, the Victory Luncheonette filled a
cramped, overlooked space on a block of industrial buildings
in Manhattan's East Village. Its founder, proprietor, and staff
were all one person: Ernie. As you might guess from the
name of the luncheonette, Ernie was a veteran of the Last
Good War, to which cause he had given his right leg.

It was nothing in particular that made me a regular at the
Victory. I simply stopped in one morning for coffee and a

buttered bagel. There was a crowd two or three deep at the counter, mostly workers from the area's small loft factories. The air was fat with smells of toasting and frying and the clamor of voices trying to rise above Bob Seeger's "Old Time Rock 'n Roll" throbbing from a jukebox in the back.

Gently angling my way toward the counter, I signaled for Ernie's attention.

Unaware that he was one-legged, I was momentarily caught by Ernie's odd but graceful movements as he worked the narrow space between grill and counter. Like a Sufi dervish, he was bobbing and sweeping in long, slow circles, cutting a bagel here, popping the toaster there, opening the coffee spigots on two cups at once, buttering a bagel with a single sweep, scrambling an egg in what looked like a dented aluminum helmet, brushing litter from the counter, cutting another bagel, flicking back the coffee spigots at the last possible moment—all the while contributing abbreviated comments to conversations with half a dozen customers. I must have been hypnotized by this performance because I suddenly found him pointing at me.

"Yastrzemski for MVP," he was saying. For the second time.

The wheels were turning slowly. I blurted back another name.

"Mantle."

"Silvio, you hear that?" He was poking at someone's shoulder. "The professa says Mantle. Yaz is a bum. What'd I tell ya?"

A small circle had formed. From the way they were looking at me, I was encouraged to think it was a Mantle crowd.

"You want something or you got all day?"

"Umm. Coffee and a buttered bagel."

"Toasted?"

I wanted it untoasted but by the time I could respond he had sliced it, rammed it under the gas flames of the grill, and turned to another order.

"Yaz can hit. I'll give you that, Silvio."

Silvio responded with a dubious shrug and started squeezing a long yellow worm of mustard onto a reeking mass of fried pastrami.

The cooking equipment of the luncheonette had been so arranged that Ernie could reach every part of it by pivoting on a single foot. Two huge coffee makers were against the wall; the sinks, cutting board, and toaster were tucked under the counter. Although he could get to either end of the counter with a single giant step, he delivered most of the food by spinning it along the counter, dangerously skirting open stacks of jelly donuts and corn muffins.

Between the stained metal tanks of the coffee makers hung a photograph of Ernie from another time and world. Dressed in pajamas and a soldier's cap, one arm around a nurse and the other awkwardly gripping a crutch, he was glaring at the camera with a young man's stern resolve to show he didn't give a good goddamn.

"You want it buttered, your bagel?"

"Right."

As I walked away with my breakfast in a little white bag, I wondered how he knew I was a professor. I was wearing my Levi jacket and jeans, and hadn't cut my hair for almost a year. The idea was precisely *not* to look like a professor. Did I look like a professor trying not to look like one?

THE REASON I didn't see the mysticism in the Victory is that in the ordinary sense there was nothing to see. The nothing was there, not in what Ernie was doing but in what he was not doing.

At first it would seem that Ernie was working while everyone else stood around. As you became familiar with the place, Ernie's work seemed to disappear. You would just stop noticing he was working. There he was, spinning in his grimy apron, no more mysterious than a toasted hard roll. He was certainly the center of everything that happened in the Victory but it was a strangely unnoticed center. It should have been obvious that he was actually preparing and serving food but it wasn't obvious.

I doubt whether Ernie knew the names of more than a few of us. But names didn't matter here. Identities had a lighter weight. To the degree that we knew each other at all, it was by our orders or our baseball teams, by the jokes we told or by the intimate details about our lives that we revealed with astonishing innocence. Even if Ernie didn't recognize you, it came to about the same thing. "What's yours, lady?" "What're you buying today, pal?"

The Victory was a place where the public and private dramas of life got equal attention. How should the jury vote in the current Mafia trial? Someone's child has pneumonia. A woman is attacked in her subway station by a twelve-year-old boy. Should the Mets trade Tom Seaver for a whole new infield? Threaded through all this was the ongoing argument about whether subway tokens would ever go as high as a buck. And often events of puzzling metaphysical significance, such as the time Yastrzemski dropped an easy fly ball, causing the Red Sox to lose a crucial game. "Yastrzemski, he just doesn't drop fly balls." But the mysticism had nothing to do with these dramas themselves. It was the weightless way they passed in and out of conversation, like moonlight striking water.

Although no one ever had what you could call a conversation with Ernie, he seemed to be in every conversation at once. If he never, or almost never, forgot your usual order and if he never finished one order before starting another, he would also never forget unfinished conversations. "Yastrzemski," he would mutter, angling his head sideways at someone who had put money on the Red Sox. "How's the kid?" he would ask another. In the Victory there was no such thing as The Last Word. Truths, conclusions, absolutes—all had about the same permanence as the steamy smells that circulated in the Victory and drifted out onto the street.

Endings were part of a larger formless tumble that started from who knows where, and would go on to who gives a damn. Buddhists have a name for it: *samsara*, the state of endless change from which nothing and no one ever escape.

If the Victory was as samsaric as all this, why was it in fact festive? It was because of the way Ernie spooned sugar into a paper cup and slammed change on the counter. Over the years his actions had been reduced to their minimum. Cutting and buttering a roll was a matter of a few effortless moves. There was no one hidden in it, doing it, as it were, from a distance. Tao-like, no one was doing anything and yet nothing remained to be done. The Victory had become what Ernie did without doing it. There was a center to all this activity; it was a still center. It's no wonder that we overlooked it. We overlooked it because there was nothing to see.

It was the nothing that made it mystical.

WHETHER ERNIE saw it this way is another question. How Ernie saw it at all is a question. He would sometimes look out at the passing traffic and say loud enough for all of us to hear, "How could I waste thirty years listening to you dumb bastards?" He talked about winning the lottery. He would collect his check, close the door of the Victory behind him forever, and visit "that place in France where the Heinies ruined my future with the Rockettes." But the words hit like moonlight.

The first time I was alerted to the mysticism of the place was the morning I stopped in for my usual before lecturing on Nietzsche in my 8:30 class on existentialism. I had been reflecting on a remark in *The Genealogy of Morals*, the book in which the Buddhist influence on Nietzsche is most palpable, that "there is no 'being' behind the doing, acting, becoming; the 'doer' has simply been added to the deed by the imagination—the doing is everything."

Just as I reached the counter, Ernie had my bagel in the toaster and was telling someone which horse he should not back in the third at Aqueduct. He cut the bagel right in front of me but I still found myself wondering, Did he do it or didn't he? There was the slicing and the move to the toaster, and then the other hand back to the coffee spigot. Was this all one movement or was it many? Was he doing something? Was there someone doing it? Was there a being behind the act doing what was done? Or was the doing everything? How could you ever tell? How would you even know that about yourself?

How much of what I do is what I am not doing? It was at this moment that I remembered Growler Grashevski.

At the beginning of the wrestling season in my junior year of high school, Coach Weaver walked me over to the schedule attached to the wall of the wrestling room. He was pressing his fingers into my right bicep as though measuring it. This is an omen, I thought.

Stabbing the schedule with a thick forefinger, he drew my attention to a date seven weeks off. It was our annual match with a high school in south Milwaukee, a wrestling power-house. His grip tightened and I could feel the blood gather in my fingertips.

"Growler Grashevski," he said with an unmistakable note of warning in his voice.

I didn't need the warning. Growler was already a legend as a football player. He got his name from the animal sounds he made while attacking the opposing team. Rising from all fours as the other team came to the line of scrimmage, he would paw the air with a guttural blast of sound. He was most famous for his diving leaps, which carried all 265 of his tightly-muscled pounds over the blockers to seize the runner whom he would take to the ground with another roar of triumph. Growler's appearance doubled attendance at high school sports events and rumors abounded that the pros already had their eyes on him.

In each of my wrestling matches during those seven weeks I had only one opponent in mind. Actually, he had taken residence in my daily consciousness. I exercised, drilled, and fought against only one person, no matter who was on the mat. My matches were taking on a dreamy quality that invited a strong response from Coach Weaver.

"Don't think, Carse!" he would yell at me during practice. "This is wrestling, boy. Thinking is for philosophy." During the matches his "Don't think" became a mantra he tirelessly chanted at me.

Despite my prayerful wish for a disabling injury or one of those dreadful infections you get from a mat burn, I found myself sitting next to Coach Weaver as he drove us to the match in Milwaukee. It wasn't a highway I saw stretching out before us but a shining ribbon of fear. Every few miles the coach would knuckle me in the thigh and silently mouth the words, Don't think.

I wrestled in the heavyweight, or unlimited, class. I weighed scarcely 190 pounds and rarely wrestled anyone less than 250. Mostly they were clownish fat boys with accidental strength and little coordination. The high moment for the audience came when they first took off their warm-ups. As for me, the relative absence of both muscle and bulk made my sudden nakedness an object of hilarity.

But all this was nothing compared to Growler. In the first place, he made his entrance into the gymnasium walking on his hands. When he reached the edge of the mat he sprang to his feet in a graceful half flip, dropped to one knee, and took a Charles Atlas pose, popping a bicep at a crowd now frantic with joy. I only elevated the din by retreating as quickly as I could to my end of our team bench.

Staring across at this remarkable specimen, I reflected on the genetic unfairness at work here. While my slender Celtic forbears were doing funny dances on their toes, probably drunk, his were pulling oak trees out of the forests of northern Europe with their bare hands, no doubt eating the bark as well. There was no comfort in the fact that our team won the preceding two matches. As the referee slammed the mat with his hand, indicating the end of the match just before mine, the crowd joined Growler in a cry for revenge. His bout with me would decide the meet.

I stood up, slipped off my jersey, and stepped to the edge of the mat. My joints were made of ice. I took the standard opening stance and looked across at Growler, who was on all fours, pawing the earth and beginning his famous roar.

At the starting whistle, Growler paused for a theatrical moment, then exploded in my direction. None of my imaginary matches with him included this move. So I quickly backed and turned. With Growler's fingertips just grazing my shoulder blades, I bolted off the mat and across the gym in the direction of our bench. I found myself looking down at Coach Weaver. His face was expressionless, even as he molded his lips to form two silent words.

We took our places again on either side of the referee. This time, Growler stepped back, crouched, and came at me in a long, soaring arc. My memory of what happened in the next three or four seconds is frozen into a series of photographic stills. Growler is airborne, about six feet above the mat. My hands are on his shoulders. I am falling backward with his momentum but my feet are still square on the mat. His body does not resist the rotating pressure of my hands; it turns like a loose propeller. My feet leave the mat. He is now under me, my chest square on his. I ride him to the earth. When we hit he takes my full weight on his rib cage. There is an inhuman sound as all the air blows out of his lungs. The referee's face is inches away as he tries to see whether Growler's back is pressed to the mat. The referee slams down his hand. There is a resounding crack. The match is over. Someone is lifting me by the shoulder.

"Let's get out of here," Coach Weaver said as he dropped my warmups over me. I looked up. The crowd was motionless and silent.

I turned as we left the gymnasium. Growler was now standing, though still sucking wildly for air, holding his hands up as though begging for an explanation of what happened.

During the ride home, no one said a word for miles. I finally looked over at the coach and asked, "Well, I did win, didn't I?"

Without taking his eyes off the road, he said in a tired and solemn voice, "Don't think, boy. Don't think win, don't think lose. Just don't think. Thinking's for philosophy."

MYSTICS OFTEN distinguish between the ego and the soul, or the ego and the self. The terms are not so important, but the distinction is. The ego is the dualist in us. It is the habit we have of seeing ourselves over and against someone else. As ego, my inwardness remains inward because it is completely closed off to you by my outwardness. As ego, my wealth, intelligence, moral goodness, social class are what they are only in contrast to the person next to me. Whether or not we are believers, we oppose the natural and the supernatural; we are here and worldly, God is there and otherworldly. In fact, belief and unbelief are strictly issues for the ego; you can't be an unbeliever unless there are some believers against whom you are an unbeliever. All such oppositions are creations of the ego.

From the perspective of soul, however, we see each opposing either/or as a conjoined both/and. We can be here only because we are not there; in this way the "here" and "there" belong together. "*That* comes from *this*, and *this* comes from *that*—which means that *that* and *this* give birth to one another. Life rises from death and death from life." (Chuang-tsu) If God exists beyond all the heavens, then God must be hidden in what is closest and most familiar to us. "When there is no more separation between *this* and *that*, it is called the still-point of Tao. At the still-point in the center of the circle one can see the infinite in all things." I can be separate from you only because at a deeper level we are joined in something inseparable. I cannot be alone alone.

The still center, the soul, does not oppose anything. Not opposing anything, it does nothing. As soul, we do not act; we are. As ego, we cope with the world, change it, arrange it, try to improve it. We cope with ourselves, too, becoming our own projects, struggling to be who and where we are not. When we become aware of the still-point in a person, of a deed that has no doer, we are aware of soul; we are in the presence of presence.

My question to Coach Weaver was the ego's question: I did win, didn't I? It had a dualism in it. It was the ego that rode to Milwaukee on a ribbon of fear. The ego's question on the return trip is telling. I'd been on the mat with Growler a mere nine seconds and my memory of that sequence of events was nearly perfect, but still I didn't know whether I had won or lost. The reason is obvious. I didn't do anything. These things just happened. My feet were on the mat. My hands were on Growler's shoulders. Growler turned like a loose propeller. There was no doer in these deeds.

What happened to the ego? Maybe it froze or died or just gave up, not caring what would happen. For some reason, it got out of the way. Whether the coach's "Don't think" had an effect I can't say. Perhaps it was the long months of disciplined practice, the endless, mind-numbing repetition of basic moves that took over and did what it did no matter what I might have been thinking. I remember what happened but I don't remember doing it. I was not watching myself, not thinking about acting, not being something outside of the act.

Coach Weaver's reaction afterward was dismaying. I expected praise, celebration, a gleeful hug, but there was not a word, never a single reference to that match. At the time I found his disinterest startling. Now, however, I am much more startled by my own lack of awareness of what I was doing in the final few seconds of that match.

When the ego steps out of the way, the soul neither wins nor loses. The soul triumphs over nothing and cannot be defeated. Nor does it comfort us in our losses. These are all matters of ego and therefore matters of indifference to the soul.

I DON'T KNOW what Ernie was thinking when he talked about winning the lottery but I do know he might have lived his life quite differently. If he had chosen to "make something" of himself, he would have acted as ego, dualistically, taking the measure of himself by what opposed him. He might then have decided that these thirty years were really a waste of time and that if he had been more adroit in a worldly way, he would now be collecting rent on this building rather than paying it to someone he had never met. Who knows, he could have had a whole chain of Victory Luncheonettes and driven a Cadillac to work. But then, if he had had such regrets, he would only have worked against himself—each roll, each cup of coffee a reminder of failure, of time forever lost. He would have been absent from the Victory—and so would his customers. Even as we stood there, we would have been somewhere else.

In spite of the sepia photograph of a brave young soldier on the wall and the nostalgia in the name of the luncheonette, Ernie wasn't trying to keep the past from passing away. The war had profoundly affected his history but he was not at war with that history. The Germans got his leg but he was not fighting its loss by trying somehow to compensate for it, proving he could act like a normal two-legged person. Had he done so, he would have still been on that battlefield, carrying that huge past with him. He was no Rockette, but no Rockette could have been more balletic, less weighted with the superfluous. He was no Rockefeller either, but no millionaire could have been more oblivious to the quantity of his wealth.

Ernie did not stand over against his history, his customers, his bagels, his nameless landlord. Because they were not opposing objects that had to be struggled with, there was an effortlessness about him. This is why he never appeared to be working. This is also why, when we walked into the place, our own struggles seemed to belong somewhere else. It was infectious. For a few moments each day, we could be who we were without having to be anyone. Ernie's effortlessness seemed to become ours. We were absorbed into the gentle chaos of the Victory, gliding with its rhythms, taking our places in the nonstop conversation. There were no boundaries between its impermanence and our own, and our lives became what they were anyway—samsaric, passing away.

Something else: because our struggle in life is inherently a struggle against samsara, and because for that brief time we did not resist the passing away, we existed in that state which Islamic mystics know as *fana al-fana*, the passing away of the passing away. Some mystics call it ecstasy. Buddhists describe it with the starkest possible declaration: *Nirvana is samsara.* Nirvana, the highest goal of the spiritual life, is identical with the impermanence of everyday life. "That which is the limit of nirvana is also the limit of samsara; there is not the slightest difference between the two." (Nagarjuna)

If we are looking for the mystical, we need go no further than the Victory, no further than the most ordinary of our ordinary experience.

Just as the sea is never without an obscuring surface, the ego never really ceases to exist. It may well be that Ernie thought most of us were dumb bastards and that if he had our legs he would sure as hell be somewhere else in life. But the thought was foam; he did not remain over against us or himself. There was no doubt something that Ernie wanted to be but there was a nothing in him that was higher than that something.

THE MYSTICISM of the Victory Luncheonette was hidden in its ordinariness—which is to say that it was revealed in its ordinariness. Mystical vision is seeing how extraordinary the ordinary is.

I saw but I didn't see that I saw. My seeing was strictly in the mode of ego. From the perspective of ego, doing by way of not doing makes no sense. It makes no sense because it has no opposing impact on the world. It has no visible effect; it changes nothing. Ernie's egoless slicing and pouring will have no place in the history of the East Village. The mystical is thoroughly worldly—nirvana is samsara, after all—but its inherent indifference to the world seems to leave the world exactly as it is.

It is true that there was something infectious in the fact that no secret doer was hiding behind Ernie's slicing, buttering, and pouring. The presence of this absence allowed each of us to enter an egolessness of our own. That is an effect of a kind. But it is hard to trace its results. Each time I walked away from the Victory, I registered, however slightly, the return of a need to be something above the ordinary. I resumed the seriousness about my own special way of doing things that I had dropped for the few minutes of my daily toasted buttered bagel and coffee. It was as though at the exit I had revived a mute yearning for fresh matches with the Growler Grashevskis of the world. One leg was enough for Ernie; two legs were not enough for me. Sure, I wanted nirvana as much as the next guy but I wanted it as a passage out of my samsara, not into it.

I am a teacher. When I enter the classroom in the usual, nonmystical way I want something extraordinary to occur there and believe it will happen if I make it happen. I do it by attempting to interrupt the familiar paths of my students' thought with well-defined but provocative ideas, whether I am teaching existentialism or the philosophy of religion or even mysticism. If I do it correctly they cannot avoid making their own thoughtful way through them. I am a classroom atheist. I advocate none of these ideas; or, perhaps, I advocate them all equally. What students choose to do with them I want them to do as freely as possible. And if you ask me whether I think my teaching makes a difference to my students, I will tell you honestly that I hope so and often believe so. In fact, I wouldn't teach if I didn't believe so.

The classroom looks very different when I take a mystical view of it. If there is anything truly extraordinary in my teaching it is found in its ordinariness. Moreover, just as the still-center of the Victory is not something Ernie did, I cannot guarantee by anything I do that there will be a still center in my teaching. As with Growler, it would have to be something that happens without my doing it, without my even noticing it.

ONE DAY I made my ritual stop at the Victory while on my way to lecture on Kierkegaard's *Fear and Trembling*. Speaking of the way Abraham was greater than all our ordinary heroes, Kierkegaard said, "One became great by expecting the possible, another by expecting the eternal; but he who expected the impossible became the greatest of all."

As soon as I stepped in the door it was clear that something was different. Ernie's back was to the counter; he was laboring over the grill in a way that made it look like work. The place was filled with the regular customers but the usual samsaric flow had been fractured; there was a dark weight in it. Before I asked, someone explained that the building had been sold and Ernie would have to vacate. Ernie pushed my breakfast onto the counter without a comment. I paid for it and left, saying nothing. I never saw Ernie again.

A week or so later, on my way to the same class, I noticed that a dumpster had been rammed against the curb just a few steps from the door of the Victory. I stopped to watch as two men pulled the splintered remains of the counter out onto the sidewalk. By the time I returned, a couple hours later, the luncheonette was empty and walls were being knocked down, filthy with years of grease and smoke. On one wall I could see a bright rectangle of unstained paint where a photograph had long been attached.

A Philosopher Needs a Cat

Abu Yazid made his periodic journey to purchase supplies at the bazaar in the city of Hamadhan—a distance of several hundred miles. When he returned home, he discovered a colony of ants in the cardamom seeds. He carefully packed the seeds up again and walked back across the desert to the merchant from whom he had bought them. His intent was not to exchange the seeds but to return the ants to their home.

A SUFI LEGEND

To be a philosopher, you need a cat," Bill said. We had just visited in my apartment and were saying good-bye at the elevator. My cat, Charlie, had followed us and was now watching as we exchanged our final words. Bill, who has a cat and is a philosopher, looked down at Charlie as though he should say something to the cat as well. But when Charlie looked at Bill, there was no sign in the cat's clear and attentive gaze that anything needed saying. It was a face free of incomprehension.

The elevator came. Bill gave the cat another thoughtful look. Charlie, however, did not move or change his expression. "See what I mean?" Bill said. The elevator doors closed.

I stood there with Charlie, wondering what to make of Bill's sutra.

Why does a philosopher need a cat? I looked down at Charlie and got the same all-seeing, unfiltered gaze. More than ever, I was aware of the lack of speech in Charlie, even the lack of a need for speech. I can see that Charlie is silent but what he is silent about, what he would say if that silence broke, I don't even know how to imagine.

"Why can't I be a philosopher without you, Charlie?" If the expression in Charlie's eyes at that moment were in a human face, it would be certain evidence of transcendent wisdom, as in the face of the Buddha. But from a human face we also expect a spoken response, especially if we see in it an intentional silence. We expect the disciplined silence of a master to issue in speech, and the deeper the silence the deeper the speech that rises from it. From the Buddha, whose face is the very image of desirelessness, empty of both comprehension and incomprehension, has come an ever expanding ocean of written and spoken wisdom.

Although Charlie's face has the same absence of both comprehension and incomprehension as the Buddha's, it does not suggest an ocean of words needing to be spoken. The animal's face warns us that we might have it backwards. Instead of the speech that comes after silence, we begin to wonder at the possibility of a silence that comes both before and after speech. Is this what Bill's sutra meant?

If so, then it is not the Buddha's face we recognize in Charlie, but the animal that gazes out through the eyes of the

Buddha. It is not accidental that the word for animal comes from the Latin *anima*, soul. The primitive practice of representing the gods as animals may not be so primitive after all. Soul is not only the "still-point of Tao" where there is no more separation between "this" and "that," it is also the presence of the unutterable within us.

ARISTOTLE DEFINED a human being as an animal having speech (*zoon echon logon*). The implication is not that we have ceased being animals but that we have risen above our animal nature by the possession of language and, with language, mind and culture. This leads easily to the view that the animals around us are inferior beings and to the companion view that the animal parts of our own human being must come under the rational (verbal) domination of our superior part (mind). Descartes is the most renowned champion of this view, taking it to a dualistic extreme not found in Aristotle: "I observe no mind at all in the dog, and hence believe there is nothing to be found in a dog that resembles the things I recognize in a mind." Just as there is nothing resembling mind in the animal, there is nothing animal-like in the mind. Unfortunately, Descartes thought, the mind is for the moment trapped in an animal body, but fortunately, it is only for the moment. Death will liberate the superior part from the inferior.

The darker implication of this familiar belief is that since animal existence belongs to death, animals are to be treated as absent of anything we recognize as life. In Descartes' mind, animals are merely mechanical, incapable even of humanlike feeling. As our humanness advances, it is therefore at the expense of the animal in us and around us.

Descartes is the philosopher of ego. By stating that ego is made of a completely different substance from all material entities, he not only sets mind into dualistic opposition to both body and world, he insists that the mind can know itself through and through. The dog has no mind because Descartes recognized nothing of himself in the dog. That is, one's own mind, one's very identity, can only be what one recognizes.

Descartes thought he was pointing to the absolute irreconcilability of two kinds of substance—mind and body. In fact, he was dividing ego from soul, but could not have understood it this way because he did not see how he could be unrecognizable to himself. It would have made no sense to Descartes to say that it is the perfect silence that makes language possible, that nothing spoken makes us human.

Unrecognizability is not to be confused with the unconscious. The unconscious is, after all, what either could be or already has been conscious. In principle it is all recognizable. The theory of the unconscious remains a thoroughly Cartesian construct. True unrecognizability is to be understood in other terms. One of the anonymous authors of the Upanishads asks, Who is it that sees, who is it that knows? "The eye of the eye, the mind of the mind," is the answer. And who is that? It is Atman, the soul of the soul. Because it is the soul that sees, that knows, it is the soul that cannot be seen or known. The soul cannot be an object of itself any more than an eye can see itself or a finger touch itself. Whatever *is* recognized, because it is an object of my attention, cannot be what I myself most am.

I recognize nothing in Charlie. I can recognize speechlessness but only a speechlessness that is a waiting or a preparation for speech. I have no acquaintance with a silence that complete in myself. If a lion could speak, Wittgenstein said, we could not understand him. Wittgenstein is not implying that if we could get to know lions well enough we could know what they are saying. This is not a failure of translation but a failure to find anything that will translate into speech. It is presence that remains presence. Pure soul. "Even if you are able to describe the Language of the Birds," Rumi asked, "how can you discern what they want to say? If you learn the call of the nightingale, what will you know of its Love for the Rose?"

DESCARTES HELD another familiar and emphatically dualistic view. The process of thought was for him merely internalized and silent speech; consequently, speech is but thought made audible. True thought is thought that corresponds accurately to objects in the world. That is, the objects are there, independent of thought and speech, and the rational thinker attaches the right words to the right objects. What cannot be thought cannot be said and what cannot be said cannot exist.

The mystics' vision is correspondingly different: "Before there were the heavens and the earth, there was the unnameable. Naming was the mother of the ten thousand things."

(Lao Tsu) There are no things until there are words to name them. The names do not, therefore, come from the things, but from the silence that precedes the act of naming.

The Taoist insight here is not that we are literally the creators of our own worlds. It is that in using language we create distinctions where none exist. For Taoists as for Buddhists and Sufis, everything is under way, in motion, passing, impermanent, samsaric. Using words to isolate some portion of the flux is like taking a photograph of the surface of the ocean. No sooner does the lens close than a different ocean appears. It may be the same ocean but no single photograph, or any number of photographs, can capture its oneness. The truly real, as the Hindus say, is *neti neti*, not this and not that. "You see the mountains," begins a Quranic saying, "you think them firm, yet they move like clouds." (Sura 27:90)

The issue for mystics is not whether we use our language accurately to describe the world that is really there but whether we see that the things created by our language have the impermanence of foam on the face of the unnameable, the unknowable, the unutterable. For Aristotle and Descartes, the silence of animals that does not give rise to speech makes them our inferiors. Mystically speaking, the opposite is true: because the animal is closer to its own silence, it is closer to God.

When I look for the unnameable within myself, I don't know what to look for. But then, I couldn't see it anyway; it is not to be seen, for it is indistinguishable from the act of seeing. What I encounter in Charlie is a speechlessness I cannot find in myself, yet it is a speechlessness that precedes speech, the world, and knowledge of the world. I cannot, of course, tell you what that speechlessness really is or is not. This is not a matter of positive knowledge about what happens in a cat's brain but the impossibility of ever knowing what it is like to be Charlie. It is just as impossible for me to know what happens or does not happen in the interior of my own being. In Charlie, I encounter an intimation of my strangeness to myself. He is a mirror to my soul that I cannot be to myself.

I first saw Charlie when he was looking out between the buttons of my son Keene's jacket. Keene had walked into my study as though he had an announcement to make. Instead he just pointed to the tiny face that was giving me a no-nonsense stare. "Where did you get that?" I asked. The question was loaded with years of more or less disastrous experience with the children and their pets. The ant colony was fine for a while; then to the children's grief the ants just disappeared leaving not so much as a single corpse behind. I took the turtle away because they refused to stop kissing it. The gerbils multiplied phenomenally until we were forced to give them away, but not before an undetermined number of them escaped into the walls or were surreptitiously released in the hallway.

"There was a lady on the street with a box of kittens," he said. "She told me to take one home for Christmas. I took this one because of its white socks."

I would scarcely have admitted it at that moment but there is something extraordinary in the ordinary practice of keeping animals as domestic companions. The unconditional love we are capable of expressing for small beings can mask but not overcome the fact that we love what we can never finally know. We can love only what cannot be fully recognized, what cannot yield its mysteries to thought. "I will leave on one side everything I can think," wrote the anonymous author of the medieval mystical classic, *The Cloud of Unknowing*, "and choose for my love that thing which I cannot think!"

I have never asked Bill what he meant by his gnomic remark. Perhaps it is enough to say that he is headed in a direction opposite that of Descartes, the great dualist and father of modern philosophy. Bill cannot be a philosopher without a cat; Descartes could only be a philosopher without a dog.

ALTHOUGH AS A CHILD growing up in Wisconsin I never met a mystic, I was of course everywhere surrounded by the mystical. The most memorable early encounters with what I would later recognize as the mysticism in the presence of animals came each March and November with the migration of waterfowl along the shores of Lake Michigan.

First, there was the lake itself: the prevailing grayness of the skies merged so perfectly with the water that the horizon vanished, giving the impression of endlessness. But there was no beauty in this infinite; there was something closer to terror in it, especially in March when slabs of ice that had broken away from the shore rose and fell with a threatening heaviness, like shoulders of the dead. Even in November the water was so cold that a swimmer couldn't survive in it for more than a minute or two. Yet, through this menacing void passed a restless river of life—ducks and geese by the million.

"Where are they going?"

"South."

"Where's that?"

"Far, very far from here."

"How do they know how to find it?"

"They just know."

"Why don't they stop here?"

"They know this isn't the south "

"Do they know this is Milwaukee?"

"Well, no, they don't know that."

"Are they lost?"

"No."

This last answer always brought a pause to the conversation. The birds didn't know where they were but they weren't lost. They knew where they were going even if they had never been there before. This is the kind of paradox that can make inquisitive six-year-olds into dialectical thinkers; that is, into truly annoying pests.

"If the birds aren't lost but don't know they're in Milwaukee," I wanted to ask, "does that mean that we are lost because we *do* know this is Milwaukee?"

If as adults we are annoyed by questions like this, it is not because they are unanswerable but because the answers raise even larger questions about the certainties that come with being adults. We know where we are but are we really so sure we're not lost?

As I got older I did the usual thing with mysteries like this. I either forgot them outright or forgot them by burying them under factual answers. As for the knot of enigmas associated with the migrations, I simply learned how to name each of the species. The first name I learned was merganser, actually red-breasted merganser. The name itself was odd enough that it stuck but the birds are odd, too. Their raked back crests give them a look of constant astonishment. Brightly marked with green, auburn, and white, they are a dressy, formal sort of bird. Best of all, they are distinctive in the air with an arrowlike flight, head extended forward as though they can't get there soon enough. Mergansers take off slowly, however, whacking the water with their wings, while the more common mallards and black ducks seem to blow right off the surface. But then the blacks and mallards are much less classy in the air; no real style in flight. Blue-winged teals were for a while my passionate favorites. Among the smallest of the migrators along Lake Michigan, they appear in compact, nervous flocks, landing and ascending on secret signals, almost invisible in the water. Much trickier to identify are the gadwalls, darkly colored, solitary birds passing silently with an air of indifference, very much unlike the showy pintails with their elegant necks, self-conscious posture, and ostentatious tail feathers.

Knowing the names of birds created an illusory sense of familiarity. And learning to identify them from their field marks and behavior, I felt I had come closer to them somehow. There were, to be sure, plenty of reminders that I still had far to go. Once I saw a hooded merganser far out of its normal range, and sometimes I would glimpse a solitary thread of geese drifting silently by a good mile above the lake. Because of their silence I could only guess they were not canadas but the smaller, more elusive brant. These moments left an ache that resembled an odd combination of both loneliness and loss. But I had the predictable response. Instead of a failure of knowledge itself, I took this to be my failure to have enough of it. The immense remoteness of these ordinary natural phenomena was merely the immensity of my own ignorance in reverse. If I could only find enough names, the placelessness of these wanderers would fall into a tidy scheme and I could finally stop puzzling over the insistent mysteries left behind.

This is, after all, a popular notion of what knowledge does for us: it eliminates ignorance. This is an exuberantly confident attitude toward knowledge. Standing on the firm ground of established fact, we can build avenues of inquiry outward, mapping the surrounding territory as we go. By these means, we will in time circumnavigate the universe. We assume we have already come far. Vast regions of ignorance have been explored, mapped, and so simply explained that even children now know what geniuses like Aristotle and Descartes could not have imagined. In this popular conception, all the secrets of a cat's mind will eventually be so thoroughly exposed they will be no more wondrous than a city map.

Whether or not such a view of knowledge is defensible, there is no denying that in practice it harbors an incipient mysticism. If the standard picture is that we are pushing back the walls of ignorance, the mystical view is that the ignorance must be there first, else there is nothing to push. The mind does not come to life until it meets what it cannot comprehend. What made the migrations irresistible to me as a child was not just that I didn't know what was happening; my mother didn't know either. That meant nobody knew. Just as a philosopher needs a cat, I needed a ragged line of wild geese in the gray November sky and the certain knowledge that no one knew what they were doing there. It was an encounter with placelessness that made me wonder for the first time if I had a place myself.

When we forget that knowledge rises from ignorance and think of it instead as a way of overcoming ignorance, knowledge can have the ironic effect of limiting our vision. Thus, the psychoanalyst who sees the world psychoanalytically, the lawyer whose life is a model of procedural orderliness, the theologian whose interpretation of Scripture is relentlessly hermeneutical, the nationalist whose heroic dreams divide the world into good and evil forces.

The wild geese do not know where they are but they are not lost. Knowledge can lift the veil. It can also become the veil. "In the pursuit of knowledge, every day something is added," Lao Tsu declared. "In the practice of the Tao, every day something is dropped." This is not mere anti-intellectualism; it is a recognition of both the importance and the limitations of knowledge. Learn what you can, then learn how to leave your learning behind you for it can hide you from the ceaseless change in and around you. The great Tao "nourishes infinite worlds, yet it doesn't hold on to them." Only by releasing our attachment, can we, in Rumi's phrase, "find our place in placelessness."

CHARLIE HAS just leapt onto my desk. On cold days he likes to lie under the heat of the desk lamp. He stretches across my work and stares at me. I can easily throw him off. He never seems disturbed when I do. But I don't and I wonder why. Is it the animal silence I share with him? Is it that I am reminded of something in myself that cannot be disturbed?

An Eye for Killing Buddhas

One morning the teacher announced to his disciples that they would walk to the top of the mountain. The disciples were surprised because even those who had been with him for years thought the teacher was oblivious to the mountain whose crest looked serenely down on their town.

By midday it became apparent that the teacher had lost direction. Moreover, no provision had been made for food. There was increasing grumbling but he continued walking, sometimes through underbrush and sometimes across faces of crumbling rock.

When they reached the summit in the late afternoon, they found other wanderers already there who had strolled up a well-worn path. The disciples complained to the teacher.

He said only, "These others have climbed a different mountain."

SOMEWHERE in a cluster of yellow birches I could hear the *zee-zee-zee*-zur-*zeet* of a black-throated green warbler. Behind me in the meadow there was a symphony of bird song, a few other warbler species along with the usual sparrows and phoebes. From this sound alone you would know this was the middle of May, the crescendo of bird migration.

It was just after dawn. I had driven up to our old house the evening before. For nearly thirty years it had been a migratory ritual of my own. I always thought of it as a way of greeting these tiny citizens of the air, hardly heavier than the air itself, as they ended their three- or four-thousand-mile journeys, flown mostly at night, precisely to these birches, this meadow, this forest. But this year it was very different.

Less than two weeks before, my wife, Alice, had died in my arms after a long and terrible struggle with cancer. As I focused my binoculars on the birches, I knew I was searching for something more than the black-throated green. It was more than a restless need for distraction that brought me here this chill and gleaming morning. But what?

In the few days since Alice's death, our thirty-seven years together had already begun to acquire the solemn permanence of fact. A boundary had been drawn, distances appeared, the time for definitions had come. I was taking the first steps back to look at a shared life in which the sharing had ended. There was this new thing in me, a history that had drawn up all its bridges. Look, it commanded, but don't enter. I was forced to see that what I had always assumed was my history was really our history. But because nothing would again be ours, what was always mine was no longer mine. The time-defying present that had been our presence to each other was now a past. It was a past that was sliding out from under me with the force of continental shift and I had not yet begun the fierce labor of staking out a new place to stand.

Partly, I needed to be reminded that the wildly impossible is possible: tiny creatures, a few ounces in weight, navigating whole continents in the dark. Although the cost to the birds is high—only a few will survive three or four of these round-trips—their ancestors sang precisely these songs, syllable for syllable, in these same forests countless millennia before the first human voice was heard in them.

As if that weren't enough, there is the impossibility of their remembering exactly where they started their journey and yet flying straight back to that place. All this with a brain smaller than an orange seed. We sometimes try to explain the inexplicable by regarding this dot of cerebral matter as a kind of onboard computer, speculating that they chart their flight path by reading the stars, the magnetic field, geological features, even distinctive regional odors, and thereby neatly sidestep the more obvious mystery. We ask how it's possible that they can find their way back to where they started when the miracle lies in the fact that they don't start at all; they just continue doing what they have always done. In our study of these impossibilities, we seem never to realize how much we have forgotten in becoming human. The birds know their way without the need for thought. But we, surrounded by thought, cocooned in it, are forever veiled from the plain seeing of earlier knowledges. Perhaps I needed now to remember that. I was hungry for the miracle of a return of my own, to a place prior to thought, and deeper.

By now I had made my way over the road and down to the edge of the pond with the dull hope that I would be visited by the old great blue heron that has long been hunting here. I leaned against the ancient stump of a tree cut by beavers decades ago. Over time this spot had acquired a history that was just my own. I sometimes came here, alone, to meditate.

If I was looking for something forgotten, it was for what had always been there beneath the retreating land mass of a concluded history. Standing on the shore of Lake Michigan as a boy and wondering at the waterfowl threading their forlorn way through the endless gray of sky and water was my first lesson in mortality. Not the birds—mine. They would do this forever; I would occupy my own space but once. My journey was from here to there; theirs was so perfectly continuous they lived in a seamless *here*. I saw then that to be human meant endlessly searching the *there* for what we could never quite attain, never even knowing what the search was for or why. I knew where I was but suddenly I was lost. The Milwaukee of my boyhood was a most precise here, but it was a here draining itself forward into the indefinite there. Now, half a century later, the question persists. Can I find my way into a zero of time where the unpredictable ravaging of these accidental histories won't touch me? Can I, as the Sufis ask, "be who I am before I was"?

Busy with these thoughts, I slid to the ground with my back to the old beaver stump. To be who I am before I was. It was an impossibility; at least it was to the rational, ego awake intelligence. To that intelligence the phrase doesn't even make sense.

I found myself sitting in my usual posture for meditation. If thought couldn't get me there, could meditation? Could I meditate my way from the pain saturating my consciousness into a deeper and probably impossible serenity? By the practice of meditation—or any other proper discipline—could I, as Rumi said, "find joy in the heart when grief comes"? Finding joy in the heart seemed, at that moment, to be as heroic a task as circumnavigating the earth to find the nest I was born in.

What made the task so difficult is that, in truth, I didn't even want to find joy. I wanted something much, much simpler. I just wanted Alice to walk down from the house, touch the back of my neck, and say, "Hi, honey." Then I wanted to sit there, her head on my shoulder until Great Blue had come and gone, until the summer had passed, until the seasons flew over each other so fast that the mountains seemed to dance and clap their hands. Instead, grief had come and had come to stay. Joy?

"MEDITATION IS in truth higher than thought," declared an anonymous rishi in the pages of the Upanishads. Then, as if knowing we would wonder what could be higher than thought, the rishi added: "The earth seems to rest in silent meditation." Whether we picture the earth resting on the back of a turtle or riding the currents of astral gravity, we still have the question of where the turtle stands or what holds the stars on course. In the Upanishadic vision the whole universe must rest in that which is nothing like itself, neither spatial nor temporal. The suggestion is that, like the earth, we can be what we are as we are only if we allow ourselves to float in meditation. But not just meditation, *silent* meditation. This is the mode of our being before speech, before thought, before action. This is a spiritual discipline that sounds more like not doing than doing. How can we pursue a discipline without pursuing it?

The mystics were fully aware of this paradox and had much to say about it. "Not everyone catches a wild ass," said the Sufi master Sharafuddin Maneri, "but only a person who is actually running can hope to catch one." Maneri was speaking of the necessity of disciplined effort in the mystical life. This remark clearly hints that spiritual discipline is something we must *do*. We will get nothing without running after it. At the same time, Maneri knew we could run and still get nothing.

Mystics say a great deal about how we are to run, but with little agreement. Prayer, seated meditation, walking meditation, guided meditation, fasting, dancing, chanting, physical isolation, living in community, acquired poverty, self-examination, concentrated study of sacred texts, long periods of silence, guidance by a teacher, a dozen varieties of yoga, sexual excess, sexual abstinence, finding the hidden meaning of numbers, pathless wandering, devoted service to others, institutional obedience—all are suggested forms of spiritual discipline. And within each of these there are any number of alternative routes. Some mystics say there are as many paths as there are seekers, others that each step is the beginning of a new path. Maybe it's true, as Catherine of Siena said, that all the way to heaven is heaven; we arrive as soon as we depart. We are left with an obvious question: so we must do something, but will anything do? Is there no deeper principle at work in the design and pursuit of a disciplined life?

If there is such a principle, it seems to appear in a widely expressed caution: every discipline harbors contradiction. We can become so focused on the path that the path becomes its own end. "For whoever seeks God in some special Way," Meister Eckhart said, "will gain the Way and lose God who is hidden in the Way." Sufis, aware of this danger, made a practice of forgetting themselves by actively remembering nothing but God. Thus developed the *dhikr*, or ritual recollection of God. But this correction of spiritual discipline soon needed correction itself, because remembering to remember can become its own goal. A true recollection of God should result in forgetting everything but God, including the recollection of God. "Those who remember His recollection," said Abu Bakr, "are more negligent than those who forget His recollection." "True *dhikr*," said Shibli, another Sufi, "is that you forget your *dhikr*."

The danger, then, is that we can become so preoccupied with the path that we do not go anywhere on it while all around us life goes on its way. Eckhart concludes his warning by remarking that "whoever seeks God without any special Way, finds Him as He really is . . . and He is life itself." But how can we seek God without having a special way to do it?

This brings us to a paradox compact as stone: Without a spiritual discipline we go nowhere, but a discipline intentionally followed may lead us only to the practice of the discipline.

It may well be that the key to this paradox lies in Eckhart's stark claim that what we are to seek is "life itself." If the disciplined life is something other than ordinary life, is it possible there is a discipline already hidden in the ordinary? Have we always been on our way toward being who we are before we were—without knowing it? Are we mystics before we try to be mystics, even before we know anything of mysticism?

As the Buddhists put it, we are all unaware Buddhas whose efforts to lift ourselves out of the ordinary hide our true natures from ourselves. The Buddhists echo Eckhart's point in the declaration that *nirvana is samsara*—the highest achievement of the spiritual life is within the full embrace of the ordinary. Like our striving elsewhere, attachment to a discipline is but our desire for the extraordinary. Our appetite for the big experience—sudden insight, dazzling vision, heart-stopping ecstasy—is what hides the true way from us. Therefore, we need a discipline that undoes our attachment to a discipline. Thus the meaning of the famous sutra, "If you meet a Buddha on the road, kill him."

But, of course, we first need the Buddha to teach us this, to teach us that we are already there, on a road of our own.

WHEN YOU NEED a teacher, the Hindus say, a teacher will appear. But we can't know in advance what we need to learn, else we would not need to learn it. Therefore, we won't know who our teachers are until we have been taught. As a result, every teaching is a surprise.

While transplanting flowers with Alice on a spring day some years ago, I was puzzling over whether to put marigolds near calendula. She shrugged casually. "All natural colors go together," she said. "It doesn't matter where you put them." This unexceptional remark, a passing observation of no intended significance, surprised me for what it hinted about the character of spiritual wakefulness: although the variety of natural things is so dazzlingly vast that no one color, sound, shape, or odor, however minute, is quite like any other, all natural things belong together just as they are. One thing leads perfectly to the next, nothing interrupts, nothing is lost. And there is a naturalness in the inner life as well. Thoughts, feelings, passions, conflicts, these too belong together just as they are. It doesn't matter where we put them either.

Stating it like this can, of course, sound nuttily permissive. It looks like a blank go-ahead for whatever we already are doing, until we realize that it is unnatural arranging and rearranging that gets us into difficulties to begin with, thus creating the need for discipline. By trying to order the garden of our lives according to some design alien to it, we find ourselves at war with its innate exuberance, its nonstop self-transformation. So let it be. Even let our war with it be. Going to war against war is, after all, the usual justification for war. Can it be that by letting boundaries be boundaries they cease being boundaries?

Alice's sutra, "All things natural belong together," helps define the goal of meditation for me. By meditating, I try to see the noises and colors peculiar to my own condition as a natural part of the whole. They are as completely samsaric as all that surrounds me. What is within and mine is quite as impermanent as what is without and not-mine. Even mine and not-mine are *fana* and will naturally pass away. Chuang

Tsu called this "hiding the universe in the universe." Unnatural, artificial, contrary acts, that is, those that can originate only in human beings, fracture the unity of the whole. My goal was to weed them out of myself.

Another teaching I did not know I needed came when I mentioned to a friend that I often meditate outdoors, usually leaning against the old beaver stump by the pond, but sometimes while walking through the woods. I admitted that there are frequent distractions in this practice, such as the time my meditation was interrupted by the song of a bird I had never before identified. I was so determined to know what this bird was that I followed it through the woods for half an hour before I could positively identify it. My friend laughed as though I had said something silly.

"Carse, don't you understand? Hearing the bird was also meditation."

I knew at once she was right but I wasn't at all sure what she was getting at. Not to seem too stupid, I looked again at what happened. As I experienced it, the bird called me out of meditation; or, rather, I called myself out of meditation to pay attention to this unlikely song. But why was that so amusing?

Then I turned it around. What if instead of viewing the situation as the vireo intruding on my state of pure consciousness I viewed it as my own meditation intruding on the purity of the bird's presence? Was the meditation itself an interruption?

Then, when I remembered Alice's sutra, I began to get what I think is a clearer understanding of my friend's reaction. If my goal is to see a perfect continuity between my own existence and all that is around me, samsara within, samsara without, then the meditation as I practiced it created a clear discontinuity. I was marking out a period of time in the day during which nothing could interfere, a nonsamsaric island in the day's flux that made it possible for me to contemplate the flux.

Even worse, by trying to weed out all the artificialities in myself, I was apparently heading for a nonsamsaric interior, an island of quiet perfection isolated from the noisy tumble of ordinary experience. I had used the meditation to draw a line between myself and life.

Sharafuddin Maneri was certainly right. Unless we are running we can't catch a wild ass. But surely he knew that the wild ass would outrun us every time. The only hope is that as we step up our speed, we will see that we are running like a wild ass. It is our self we run from.

GREAT BLUE glided in over the tree tops and backwinded briefly above the pond. Hanging there for a lazy moment as though he had all morning for it, he lowered his feet into a thick band of marsh marigolds at the edge of the water. I slowly picked up my binoculars. Training on his eye, I saw more than I expected. Lidless, unblinking, passionless, looking at nothing but seeing everything, this was an eye for killing Buddhas.

I put the binoculars down and stared back. A space opened between us. There was a silence of bird song and I became aware of the near mute buzzing, ticking, humming, zizzing, scratching of smaller beings. All things belong together just as they are. . . .

"Hey, Carse," Alice yelled, "I think this is yours." She was standing at the other end of the common room at the divinity school. I turned toward her just as she finished an exaggerated windup, rocked back on her right foot, and threw a projectile into the air with a mighty sweep of her arm. As it began its ascent on a long arc through the hundred feet separating us, I recognized the orange I had been nervously fingering in the dining hall where we had just had lunch together.

This had been my third encounter with Alice and as soon as I saw the orange leave her fingers I knew it would end with as much surprise, mystery, and pain as the previous two.

I had first met her a couple of weeks earlier, just before the beginning of the term, at a reception for new students. We were stiffly naming our hometowns, undergraduate colleges, and vocational expectations to second- and third-year students polite enough to seem to care, while trying to balance punch glasses and crackers gooey with cheese drooling into our hands. It was a severe test, especially for those like me who were still trying to formulate vocational expectations for ourselves. I was edging toward the door, trying to find a place to get rid of the cheese, when without warning the door opened and my life changed. She did nothing more than walk through the door, and straight at me, just because I was the first one in her path.

"Hi," she said brightly, waiting with amused impatience for me to introduce myself.

I stared down at her name tag. The best I could do was read her name out loud. "Alice."

"No, not Al-liss," she replied, correcting me sharply. "Ah-leese."

"Ah-leese?" I said helplessly.

"Not *AH-leese* and not *Ah-LEESE*," she instructed, with just a trace of European accent. "Ah-leese. Just pronounce Alice in French and you have it."

"Ah-leese," I tried again. She responded with a brief but emphatic nod and turned to the others, leaving me with all the symptoms of brain fever.

A few days later I was in the parking lot talking to Bill Coffin about his motorcycle, an Indian Scout. It seemed he had used this machine, or one like it, for espionage missions in eastern Europe after the war. He was bouncing gently on the seat, the engine popping under him, and was midway through the narrative of one of his amazing adventures when he looked over my shoulder and broke into a sudden smile. I turned to find Alice walking toward us in her usual near-run pace. I could tell from the way she was tossing her briefcase that she was ready for anything.

"Coffin," she sang out. "Take me downtown." Without waiting for a response, she pulled back her skirt and slid onto the back of Bill's seat. Bill kicked back the stand, revved the motorcycle into a numbing roar, and yelled over his shoulder, "Fest dich halten, Liebchen!"

"Hoopla!" Alice laughed as the Scout rocketed toward the back end of the parking lot. In my memory the motorcycle actually left the ground as it went over the edge of the steep hill behind the divinity school. I ran to the lip of the precipice, certain there would be a long trail of wreckage. But there they were, already halfway down, bucking along the serpentine footpath, throwing off clouds of gravel. More than anything else I remember Alice, one arm around Bill, the other expertly swinging her briefcase to keep balance, as though the two of them did this every day. Seconds later they reached St. Ronan Street and were gone. The last terrible image is of Alice's long black hair blowing straight back. *"Fest dich halten, Liebchen?"*

And then that lunch. Impelled by despair as much as courage, I joined a table of upper-class students sitting around Alice. She was talking as I sat down with my tray and she looked at me only once, blankly acknowledging me. Her fingers made intricate designs in the air as she spoke. I couldn't make my mind listen to her words. Coffin spoke German with her, I kept thinking. They probably speak French with each other as well. And that skirt. My God, she pulled her skirt back when she jumped on behind him. I attacked an orange with my thumbs, absently trying to find a way into it. What did she have on *under* that skirt? The orange was rapidly transforming itself into a bruised and leaky glob.

It was this very object speeding in my direction through the stunned emptiness of the common room. I took a few quick steps toward the end of the room and leapt, arching back as if to catch a football. Instead, I only tipped it with my fingers in a way that propelled it into a second high arc. With a decisive splat it hit the wall just to the left of a portrait of

Jonathan Edwards, the most renowned graduate of the divinity school and author of that classic work of terror, "Sinners in the Hands of an Angry God."

The stain from the orange was still visible when Alice and I were married in that same place three years later, two days before graduation. . . .

GREAT BLUE took two slow-motion steps toward the center of the pond. Picking up the binoculars, I looked again into that lidless killer's eyes and know I would never know how much was lost.

ONE EVENING at dinner, Alice related the story of the teacher who took his disciples on a desultory trek to the top of a mountain. She said she thought she might use the tale the following day in her class in Asian religions. She asked me to discuss an interpretation with her.

I thought about the story a moment."Well, I think the point of the story is pretty obvious," I said. "It's simply a parable on the transforming effect of the journey on the travelers. The point here seems to be that the more difficult the path, the more it transforms."

"So you think the effort by itself explains the difference?"

"It explains some difference," I said. "Remember how we felt when we hiked to the top of Mt. Washington with heavy backpacks and saw people who had driven up with stickers on their cars saying THIS CAR CLIMBED MT. WASHINGTON?"

"We felt superior."

"Well, yes, I suppose we did."

"Not only that," she said. "We *knew* we would feel superior to the car crowd even before we started the hike. So in that case the effort didn't change anything, it only confirmed what we felt to begin with. Maybe we even busted our bottoms for no other reason than to prove what we already thought about ourselves."

"OK. So this is not what the teacher had in mind. We knew what was going to happen, the students didn't know."

"The students were lost; in fact, they thought the teacher was lost. There they were: no trail, no lunch, and no explanation from the teacher."

"They had to be lost, didn't they?"

"The way I see it," Alice said, "they had to be lost—and confused. We knew before we went up Mt. Washington what would happen, so we learned nothing doing it. For the students, the whole thing had to be a waste of time, a cost they didn't want to pay. I mean they really had to lose something without knowing why."

"The role of the teacher is absolutely crucial here, isn't it? When we lose something without knowing why, we don't necessarily learn anything from it. Mostly we just try to keep it from happening again."

"Sure, the students didn't know it was a different mountain until the teacher told them. It became a different mountain *only* when he told them."

"That's interesting," I responded. "The teacher did nothing more than tell them what they had done and it changed the way they viewed their lives."

Alice thought for a moment. "So then would you say a teacher is anyone who leads us to a new vision of our lives just where we thought there was only loss?"

"That's the point of this story at least."

"That's not the point you first thought it had."

"Alice, are you my teacher?"

"If I said yes, I wouldn't be, would I?"

Then she laughed in that same free, joyous voice I first heard when the orange hit the wall near Jonathan Edwards.

ABOUT A MONTH before Alice died, I had a hospital bed placed in the living room of our apartment so she could sit up a little and look out at the city. One evening, as I sat at the bottom of the bed massaging her feet, we started talking quietly in an abstract way about death. I thought briefly of quoting the mystics on the subject of dying but theirs was such a hard truth for me that at the moment I couldn't bring myself to it. Alice had no particular interest in mysticism anyway.

She was silent for a while, as though reflecting, then said, "You know what I have learned about myself, about life, from these months of illness, especially now that I know I won't survive it?"

She paused to sip from a cup of fennel tea sweetened with honey, the only kind of food she could now take, and I looked up at her.

"What?"

"Nothing," she said. "Not a goddamn thing."

I knew exactly what she meant. Or thought I did. For nearly a year and a half she had fought off death. Hard. But now it was only weeks or days before death would step between us. So this is what it comes to. Nothing. Yes, I could agree with that. It made a lot more sense than the mystics.

Then I looked again at her face. There was almost no expression in it, but no tension either. Then I saw the slight smile in her eyes. Clearly I hadn't got it. I realized suddenly that it was the ego in me that had been listening, still regarding it all as a matter of struggle, seeing death as something that stood over against us, as a hostile force we needed to oppose. But Alice had moved beyond the struggle and was speaking from another place. The words "Not a goddamn thing" suddenly took on the complexity of a sutra—a mere thread of a remark, but one that can be pulled and pulled.

There had been a lot of war in her history, in her childhood no less than in her recent history, but what I saw now was that she had put down all her arms and come home. She neither needed nor wanted to be anywhere else. Her life in that lucid moment meant nothing else other than what it was. I felt the effortlessness in her. It was the unmoving center, it was soul, pure presence. I thought of Blake's hard lines:

He who binds to himself a joy
Does the winged life destroy;
But he who kisses the joy as it flies
Lives in eternity's sun rise.

Alice's presence in that moment was the presence of winged life. But the ego in me was still armed for the fight against time. I couldn't keep her alive but maybe I could bind myself to a joy and keep this moment.

It was only after a long reflection on the way this brief sutra was woven into our life together that I began to see that the moment was what it was only because she was not holding on to it.

Later I saw something else. She did not say these words to herself or to the emptiness. She said them to me. She was looking at me when she said them. It was something important for me to know. That's why when she said them, even before I had pulled at the thread, I was aware that the thirty-seven-year journey of our life together had changed in a way that would take years more to understand. It had just become an unspeakably different life.

A kingfisher let loose its terrifying shriek just behind me as it approached the pond in a long descending circle, then dropped abruptly, almost at a right angle, into the water. As soon as it hit, it was out of the water and off, something silver flashing in its beak. A drama of beauty and death, over in seconds.

Great Blue's omniscient eye gave away nothing.

A Higher Ignorance

I will teach you the best way to say Torah: not sensing yourself at all, only as an ear listening to how the world of speech
speaks through you. You are not yourself the speaker. As soon
as you begin to hear your own words, you should stop.

DOV BAER, THE MAGGID OF METZTRICH

USELESS PASSION," that's about all human existence comes to, Jean-Paul Sartre wrote at the end
of *Being and Nothingness*. I was in a mood to agree,
as I made my deliberate way through the long rectangles of
morning light expanding into Washington Square Park.
Sartre's doleful, walleyed face looked out at the same scene
from the dust jacket of the book loosely tucked in my coat
pocket. I was headed toward my eight-thirty existentialism
class.

"Freedom is the way human beings put their past out of
play by secreting their own nothingness," he said, then explained for six hundred pages how the nothing makes human
existence possible and yet at the same time produces an anx-
iety in us so unendurable that we long to fill the nothing
with something. But filling the nothing with something is an

attempt to become what we are not. This attempt is the basis of our unrelieved inauthenticity.

"Yo, Carse, man." I looked back into the face of a student from the class as he took a few fast steps to join me.

"Morning, Andrew."

Andrew shook out his hair a few times and began tying it back into a ponytail. I had the slightly embarrassed sense that he was still in the process of dressing for the day. An edgy silence passed. I felt an encounter coming.

"Carse, man," he began with a low-energy drawl that confirmed the feeling. "You know what students say about you?"

What students say about me? A small alarm rose. What was he getting at?

"Not really."

"Just don't start believing it, man."

Believing what?

"I mean, if you start believing what they say about you, you become bullshit. You understand what I'm saying?"

I looked at him blankly.

"But if you *don't* believe it," he went on, "you're there, you're real, man."

"It sounds like you have a paradox there, Andrew," I said, hoping to shift this exchange from content to form while I flipped through the possibilities in his remark: If I knew how others saw me, I'd be in danger of seeing myself in that way. If I saw myself in that way I'd not be what others saw me to be.

"Paradox. Right. That's part of what they're saying. You love paradoxes, man."

So?

Andrew stopped and faced me. Another silence. "I won't be in class. I got something to do." He gave me a power handshake, locking forearms with me, our faces inches apart. "Just . . . be careful. You know what I'm saying?" He stepped back, saluted me with a raised fist, and walked off.

Eight-thirty is an early hour for a class. Students are several levels below full consciousness, but this gives a teacher certain advantages. For one thing, since classes last an hour and a quarter, it is a lot to ask twenty-year-olds to sit in one place without moving for seventy-five uninterrupted minutes unless they are partially asleep. For another, their critical faculties are still dozing. Ideas will be entertained before the danger of thinking them has become apparent. This is especially important when the idea is that human reality is "by nature an unhappy consciousness with no possibility of surpassing its unhappy state."

I had prepared well. This was a lecture I was eager to give. I didn't want to describe Sartre's thought, I wanted to sell it. I was about to enter a room with 150 as of yet unclosed minds and load them with a fistful of subtle but angry thoughts. I was infected with a spirit of revenge. I couldn't forget what had happened at the Victory. In fact, I had begun to see a parallel between Ernie and myself. Just as the world couldn't take the time to notice the small perfection of Ernie's effortlessness, neither did it much notice the delicate subtleties in what I was about to teach.

At that moment, the class had become the world and I was going to call its attention to its boorishness, its incuriosity, its offhanded cruelty. The students' egos were mostly still slumbering, but mine was at high noon.

I unfolded my lecture notes and flattened them out next to Sartre's book. After leafing through them briefly, I looked up at the first few students making their somnolent way into the classroom and felt an odd discomfort. Andrew's remark, like a time-released potion, was beginning to take effect. I could see myself looked at. I saw I was in the role of professor, about to give a performance of Sartre's angry thought. I saw how seriously I had taken on the role.

Suddenly nervous, I looked down at the lecture notes again and found Sartre staring back at me from the cover of his book. I looked away but his gaze followed me. It was those weird eyes, one looking straight at you, the other at something else as though he saw you but also saw something you didn't see. There is a touch of amusement in them also, an expectation that you won't get it. So what was I missing?

Then I got the joke, although it wasn't all that funny. I was about to make myself a perfect example of Sartre's analysis of the way human actions inevitably become inauthentic. I was ready to fill the great nothing with what I knew was just the perfect something. I would become a comic strip version of what Sartre calls "bad faith": knowing you are acting inauthentically but intentionally forgetting that you know—like seeing two things at once but deciding not to look out of one eye.

It was a perfect postmodern moment. I was about to do to my students with this lecture the very thing the lecture urged them not to do. Like all postmodernists, I was left with two choices: I could go on as planned, contradicting myself as slyly as possible, or I could admit to the contradiction, making the class a throwaway example of the impossibility of direct, factual communication.

The room was filling. Students were coming through the door by the elevator load. An angular, stick-thin youth with hair falling around his face in long wet ribbons took a seat near the pillar in the middle of the room. He leaned dangerously forward trying to find his mouth with an open container of coffee. I remembered meeting him on the street once when he asked what experience I'd had with out-of-body travel. I also remembered he was carrying three spiral notebooks labeled SHIT ONE, SHIT TWO, and SHIT THREE.

I tried to concentrate on my lecture, scrolling it before an inner eye. It had a tight structure with beginning, middle, and end, and there were a half dozen amusing illustrations I had used before with effect. But the imminent necessity of delivering it, *performing* it, had suddenly rendered me dumb. The only way I could speak these things was as someone I was not.

I encouraged myself with the thought that, after all, I really did believe these things. Then I recalled Sartre's withering observation that "if you believe, you know you believe, and if you know you believe, you can't believe." Bad faith, again.

Sitting in the front row was a fiercely awake young man, grandson of an orthodox rabbi, who had recently converted to Christianity and taken up with a shrill band of street preachers. Sitting near him was a woman whose sister, a senior at

Radcliffe, was comatose in a Boston hospital having walked out a window while under the influence of a mind-expanding drug.

A variety of solutions played through my mind. I had prepared this lecture so well I could have simply typed it out and had my assistant place a copy of it on each desk before any of the students arrived. Better yet, I could have mailed it to them so they could read it at their leisure. In fact, I could have sent them the whole course as soon as they registered. Why was I here at all?

There is surely a difference, it occurred to me, between reading a lecture and hearing it delivered. But would it be possible to write something into the printed text that would compensate for the absence of the teacher? What can the teacher do that a written document cannot? The teacher can respond to questions the students might have. But then, one could anticipate every reasonable question and write the lecture to cover them. The teacher can display a certain attitude of seriousness toward the subject or commitment to the truth that might have an effect on students. But then, a subtly written lecture could also do this. There is a kind of energy a teacher can give the material, stimulating the students' interest or curiosity. But a clever writer could get this into the text with verbal flourishes and catchy metaphors. Still, there is something about the absence of the teacher that simply can't be accounted for in the written text. I was surprised to find there was no way of saying what exactly the presence of the teacher meant to the teaching.

There is no doubt that a kind of teaching does occur when the student is exposed only to a text. The printed words of Socrates and the Upanishadic rishis can always instruct. It is clear, however, that if we were face-to-face with these masters, something would be added to the teaching that we cannot find in the text. This must be why so many spiritual traditions stress the personal transmission of a teaching from one living voice to another. Buddhist and Hindu teachers often trace back the lineage of their masters many centuries. The apostolic succession in Christianity assumes that one can be addressed by those who were addressed by those who . . . were addressed by Jesus himself. The critical point here is that the presence of the teacher adds something to the teaching that cannot be stated—either by the teacher or the student. Moreover, it is exactly what is not said and cannot be said that constitutes the core of such teaching.

It may well be that every word that passes between teacher and student is intelligible to both. Still, in genuine teaching the teacher cannot say what is being taught nor can the student say what is being learned.

The unspeakability that confronts us here is not mere ignorance. Ignorance always implies there is something knowable but as yet beyond our reach. This unspeakability points toward an absolute limit to that which can be spoken. It is what Eckhart called a "higher ignorance." It is knowing that from within the unfinished circle of our present knowledge there is no way of knowing what keeps that knowledge forever incomplete. It is the awareness that even the simplest of our certainties are laced with mystery and surprise. "*This* ignorance," Eckhart said, "does not come from lack of knowledge but rather it is from knowledge that one may achieve this ignorance."

Several more elevator loads had wandered into class. The room was now about half full. On the pillar in the center someone had scrawled in large, careless letters: YOU ARE PAYING $18.40 AN HOUR TO SIT HERE AND DIE.

THE MYSTICAL can occur in almost any meeting between student and teacher, but there is a kind of teaching that need not be mystical. There are many knowledges and many ways of teaching them. I am concerned here with just two, each quite different from the other. One is positive, concerned entirely with fact. It relates directly to the world. It can be true or false. It has content, weight, significance. We can disagree about it and we can also resolve our disagreement by referring to matters external to us. The effect of radiation on certain cancers, troop movements at the battle of Jena, voting patterns in California, Sartre's theory of consciousness—all are matters of positive knowledge. They can be stated accurately and stored in books and computers, even passed from one tape recorder to another. We cannot live without such knowledge.

Concerning the importance of positive knowledge, I recalled the recent visit of a former student who had dropped by to report on her progress at medical school. "My grades aren't all that bad," she said, as a canny way of informing me that her brilliant undergraduate performance continues. She was then in her third year and about to make decisions that would determine her professional future. I thought at first she had come for help in thinking through her options. But it was soon obvious she had sorted out all this quite clearly.

With some animation she recounted in detail a common practice among her fellow medical students. They never missed the first class of a large lecture but their purpose in being there was not to take notes. Immediately after the lecture they organized into groups of about a dozen to arrange a schedule by which each of them in turn would tape the lecture for the others. By the second or third class, attendance dropped from about a hundred to a mere handful. The image that amused—or perhaps horrified—her the most was that of the professor reading off a lecture to a large auditorium empty of all but about ten tape recorders, each placed there by a student who was now napping, reading the paper, or across the street having breakfast in a coffee shop. Once, on her designated day, she was astonished to find that the professor, unable to attend, had sent in a tape with an assistant to be played to the machines present. And no one found this strange.

I was alarmed by the story but not in the way I would have expected. I found I was hoping only that all these machines were operating correctly, that each student was able to learn word-for-word exactly what the professor was saying. She was probably trying to tell me that the unspeakable was missing in this experience. But, it came to me now, I wished I had told her it was only by way of the speakable that she can become a physician. For it is not whether she can achieve a higher ignorance in the process of her medical education that concerns me, but whether she can sufficiently overcome a lower ignorance to be a competent professional. As a human being, of course, I want nothing more for her than a continuing quest for the higher ignorance, yet I somehow failed to make it clear how important the direct communication of ordinary, positive knowledge can be.

The other knowledge, the kind she implied was missing in her medical education, can be referred to somewhat loosely as negative knowledge. Some call it *apophatic knowledge*. An apophasis is a kind of double negative as in "my grades aren't all that bad." This is not the same as saying "my grades are terrific." The former has a nuance, a suggestiveness, a hint of subtlety that escapes the latter and, more important, cannot be said directly. When the Sufis speak of the seventy thousand veils separating us from the Divine, they are making a kind of positive claim. It is a fact that we do not have direct knowledge of God. When, on the other hand, they say that these veils are themselves the creation of God, and therefore reveal just as they conceal, they are speaking apophatically. Their apparent aim is to draw our attention to something we cannot know as a matter of positive knowledge: the limitations of positive knowledge. It is not what we don't know but what we do know that limits us. But apophatic knowledge is scarcely limited to the question of the existence of God. When Wittgenstein, for example, says that we cannot see the end of our own field of vision, the implication is that if our vision were not limited we could not see at all (to see everything is to see nothing in particular). And yet, we cannot see that which makes our seeing possible. This, too, is apophatic knowledge. There is a mysticism in ordinary vision.

Without direct, positive, informational knowledge, it is impossible to live at all. Without apophatic knowledge, it is impossible to be human. Before my former student can be a competent physician, she must accumulate a great deal of knowledge she *knows* she has. But unless she knows that there is something about her patients, herself, life, that she knows she does not know and can never know, she can approach us only as one tape recorder approaches another: absently. There can be a mysticism in the practice of medicine.

BY 8:40 THEY were mostly in the classroom. It was obvious, however, that they too were somewhat absent. Many had coffee and were sipping at it, sometimes not even bothering to lift the paper cups off their desks. The cigarette smoke was heavy. Some were clearly losing the struggle to keep their eyes open. Near the back several were in each other's arms with the bored look of waiting out an interruption.

Although there were 150 students in the class, I was familiar with many of their personal stories. It was the early seventies, when the informality of university culture meant you often knew more about students' lives than you needed or even wanted. One of them, now crossing and recrossing his legs and making repetitive, ritual movements with his fingers and eyes, was a student who had confided to me that he had sexual feelings in only the left half of his body. Another student, a woman whose identity I didn't know but could guess, had begun her last term paper with the phrase, "The other night, after I finished masturbating . . ." There were also a few older students whose expressions seemed to suggest that for what they paid in tuition dollars, this lecture had better be worth it. Then, here and there were students of such wakeful intelligence and attentiveness that it was difficult not to lecture only to them.

"Consciousness is a being such that in its being, its being is in question insofar as this being implies a being other than itself." I had wanted to start with this remark. But what was it exactly I wanted to start saying? Perhaps I could share my brief meditation about the unspeakable. But speaking about the unspeakable would likely hinder it, not produce it. Or I could just drop all references to existentialism and lecture on the importance of a higher ignorance. But you can't talk someone into ignorance. Maybe it would be better to begin laying out tracks of positive knowledge into Sartre's writings and see where they led. But I had no energy for anything this boring. I stared out at the class, unable to begin.

Then I thought of Katz—the teaching hero of my undergraduate years. I knew what Katz would do. I saw him do it in the most unforgettable class of my entire student career.

KATZ HAD ENTERED that day as he usually did, by the door at the back, walking the length of the classroom, lecture notes tucked under his arm. We always expected his lectures to be full of surprise, leaving us with much to puzzle over later, but we could hardly have foreseen what was about to happen. It started off vintage Katz. He came up the center aisle, leaning forward in the strange way he did, like he was fighting his way into a windstorm of unfinished thought, expecting danger.

As always, we were swept into the drama of a Katz class. He would reach out for the lectern as though it were a place of safety, taking firm hold of both sides. What little hair he had was combed into dark stripes just above his ears. He always wore a tie and used all three of the buttons on his sport coat. He would open class with a series of remarks that blew by too fast to catch. Instead of taking notes, we seemed to be taking shelter, wondering whether he would ever be able to hold us steady in this running sea.

Each Katz lecture was an adventure. As idiosyncratic as he appears from this distance, we never thought of him as having a particular style. He always started the semester with a threatening stack of syllabi, which he casually dumped into the lap of a student at the front of the class as he made his way to the lectern. The syllabus was an esoteric document containing alternative descriptions of the course, long lists of books that may or may not be related to the subject matter, no trace of assignments, all full of erasures and typos, clearly a work in progress. As we distributed this weighty mass among ourselves, he would open his notes, look fiercely out at nothing, introduce himself by saying only, "Katz," and start lecturing.

As each class went along, he slowly gathered his ideas into a coherent whole, and before it was over we would have taken pages of notes, scarcely noticing that in this nonstop flow of words he had abandoned the lectern and was pacing the aisles, sometimes talking from the back of the room or leaning against the window staring out. If we looked up at all, we noticed that his jacket had come off and often his tie as well. His hair would be flying loose, framing his head like an aura. Occasionally we would find him standing above us, studying the marks in our notebooks like they were esoteric runes that held the secret to it all. He might even pick up someone's notes and read a line or two to the class, but never with ridicule, always with respect, as though there were something uniquely revealing in it.

At the beginning of the term, a few bold students would dare to ask a question, but because they were usually in search of clarity the questions themselves weren't too clear. Katz would turn to the questioner and take a stance that suggested he had just been physically assaulted and was about to attack in return. We soon learned, though, that when he attacked it was his own thought that was targeted. He seemed to love the unfinished questions the best, using them to find the ragged patches in his own thinking. He never answered questions directly and would sometimes rephrase them in a form that barely resembled the original, but we noticed that our questions created in him new areas of reflection he could not have entered without us. His lectures fed on interruption. We felt powerful after these exchanges. We also felt Katz's power.

Class ended not when the bell rang but when Katz stopped talking. He would tuck the notes under his arm, study the floor around him as though something were missing but he wasn't sure what, make his way to the back, still swimming in thought, pause to look out into the corridor, then dive into it and disappear.

On this day, however, something else happened. He folded out his notes as usual, raced through a series of predictably confusing reflections, then stopped. Just stopped. He looked into the space just above our heads. No one moved. Our pens froze. Later some people said it lasted ten minutes, at least five. But there was no saying how long it lasted because time too was suspended.

He gathered his notes, tucked them under his arm, said softly, "I'm sorry, I'm empty," and left the classroom.

The notes from those classes I threw away years ago and from this distance his ideas don't seem particularly memorable. Those four words, however, are memorable. I knew when I heard them that I wanted nothing more than to be a teacher myself. In an instant, I was in a different college; I was a different student.

I STARTED writing sentences from Sartre onto the blackboard. "Freedom is the way human beings put their past out of play by secreting their own nothingness." "Nonbeing lies coiled like a worm in the heart of being." Above the blackboard was more graffiti. YOU CAN ACT YOUR WAY INTO A NEW KIND OF THINKING BUT YOU CAN'T THINK YOUR WAY INTO A NEW KIND OF ACTING.

When I turned back to the class I could see that a sort of nonexpectant silence had fallen over them. They weren't waiting for me to say something; they just had nothing to say to each other. No one was looking at me; they could not have guessed I was in an intellectual dead calm.

When I was a boy, sailing my dinghy along the shore of Lake Michigan, I used to wonder why you couldn't equip each sailboat with a fan that would drive the sails when the wind failed. Now that no ideas were rushing at me with their own energy, I had a choice. I could supply the energy myself, puffing out words that make plenty of sound but propel us nowhere, or I could do what Katz did: declare myself empty and walk out.

Then the paradox hit. By repeating what Katz said, I would not say what he said. When he made that remark, he was repeating nothing, quoting nobody. The words were his own, spoken from a still center, original, perfect. To do what he did, I could only speak from my own center, say what only I could say.

Katz was a mystical teacher. He said those four words in such a way that what he left unspoken is more than I can exhaust in an entire career of teaching. It is essential to the mysticism of that act that it was not intended to have some kind of effect on us. He didn't give a damn whether it had an effect. There was nothing more to it than that he was empty, said so, and left. He did not, in other words, use the nothing as something. What he said was not words. What he really said was nothing I or anyone else could ever say again. It was the unsayable that we heard in his talk. Therefore, the nothing was everything.

HOW DOES ONE become a teacher? How could anyone learn to teach as Katz taught? If it is the unspeakable that accounts for the teaching, what could be said that points the way to being a teacher? Can anyone teach us to teach?

A revealing feature of the secular teaching tradition in the West is that it places its origin in Socrates, the author of no known text. It is not what Socrates taught but his method of teaching that is the originating element. Yet there is no saying exactly what the Socratic method is. It is usually described as a way of teaching that consists simply in asking questions. He does ask questions but he also harangues, jests, orates, speculates, cites the gods, questions the gods, chafes at the power of his personal demon, obfuscates, mocks, contradicts himself, flatters, sneers, wanders from his subject or ignores the subject he claims to be discussing. There is no method visible in any of this unless it is a kind of anti-method. What Plato has described is a series of encounters between Socrates and his friends, or enemies, so complicated and nuanced that by the time we have abstracted from it a pattern of behavior we can emulate, we have lost its uniquely Socratic character. Plato has given us a teacher so singular as to be inimitable.

What we see in Socrates is not a developed philosophy but an engaged receptivity, an active listening. If there is anything resembling a method here it is his attempt to raise insights in his students of which he himself was incapable. In other words, Socrates' originality consists in his ability to originate in others what he could not originate in himself.

We know we have met such a teacher when we come away amazed not at what the teacher was thinking but at what we are thinking. We will forget what the teacher is saying because we are listening to a source deeper than the teachings themselves. A great teacher exposes the source, then steps back. Great teachings have all the qualities of samsara. They pass away. As soon as we hear them they are gone and we are listening to what follows. That is why we need to remember nothing of what Socrates actually taught.

For that reason, no subject matter is privileged over another. All studies in which the origins of thought point beyond themselves to deeper origins are sacred studies. Those we call teachers may or may not be teachers. Those around whom surprising thinking emerges are teachers.

A WIND must have come up. I was distantly aware that I was under way with Sartre's ideas, riding them into unexpected areas of reflection. But I was also vaguely aware that a new spirit of listening had animated the class. The notetaking was lively. The ego-driven self-consciousness provoked by Andrew's words and Sartre's stare seemed to have vanished. If any ego did remain, it was bobbing harmlessly on the rush of ideas as they tumbled over each other with an energy of their own. Pacing the room, I could feel the deeper teacher speaking through me and I became aware of the unspeakability reaching beyond. Then I began to be confident my teaching was making a difference, that maybe the world can be made to notice.

It was one of those precious moments in the exercise of any art or sport or profession when you know your skill and training are at maximum use. Aristotle's word for this was *excellence:* expressing your highest talent to its fullest measure. There is no implication here that someone else could not do what you do better. In fact, all comparison and competition disappear in these moments. It is simply that neither you nor another is in your way.

I came around the back and down the center aisle where the large pillar passed through the room like its axis mundi. Leaning against the pillar, I looked down at a student's open notebook. I recognized it at once as SHIT TWO. The pages contained nothing but neat columns of numbers from one to seventy-five. Instead of taking notes, he was staring intently at the second hand on his watch, not aware that I was only inches away. The numbers from seventy-five to forty-five were already crossed off. He X-ed out another as I watched. Forty-four minutes to go.

What would Katz have done? How could I let this response open the circle of my thought to new reflection? Should I take this as an esoteric mark revealing something surprising about the teacher or the teaching? Is it a comment on Aristotle's idea of excellence? Did it sometimes happen that Socrates spoke and no one listened? Does the unspeakable sometimes work in hidden ways? I had prepared well but how could I have prepared for this?

Forty-three . . .

The Way the Soul Sees

As soon as I attained to His Unity I became a bird with a body of Oneness and wings of Everlastingness, and I continued flying in the air of Quality for ten years, until I reached an atmosphere a million times as large, and I flew on, until I found myself in the field of Eternity and I saw there the Tree of Oneness . . . And I looked, and I knew that all this was a cheat.

ABU YAZID BISTAMI, KNOWN AS BAYAZID

THE NIGHT BEGAN with my first cup of coffee and ended with my first mystical vision. It wasn't exactly a cup of coffee, though, it was a glass milk bottle of coffee, and there was a double significance to the coffee on this occasion.

For one thing, drinking coffee had always seemed an exclusively adult matter. Cigarettes, alcohol, and sex may be the official adult prerogatives but they are different from drinking coffee. By stepping over the ritual line that marks them off, you could prove to yourself and others you were grown up. But coffee had no ritual or moral weight; it was a symbol of nothing. You didn't drink it to act like an adult; you simply drank it when you became an adult. Although at fifteen I could have ordered coffee anywhere without eliciting so much as a glance, it was a boundary to childhood I would not have dreamed of stepping over before leaving childhood itself.

Therefore, when Phil gave me the bottle full of the coffee he had just made, there was not a hint of ceremony. There was no knowing look that passed between us. There was nothing about the moment that I could ever brag about, no bravado or daring. I just stood there trying to figure out how to hold the damned thing without burning my fingers and without revealing my shock at slipping into adulthood without the least preparation.

The other significance of this memorable event was that Phil Azarian made the coffee for me. Phil was seventeen, two years older, and had something of a reputation for his singular talents. He could ride a unicycle, sign his name with both hands, and read a sextant. In sailing class, he was the only one who knew the stories of the Greek gods for whom the constellations are named. Partly for these reasons, and partly because he always wore the same serious expression and rarely spoke, adults instinctively trusted him. The principal put him in charge of the cash register at the school cafeteria, and the sailing instructor always had him check our written answers to hypothetical navigation problems. I could never tell whether he saw me as a friend, a younger brother, or a general pest. He never addressed me by name, calling me only "Kid," or sometimes "the kid."

So what did Phil mean when he handed me that bottle of coffee so easily that I wouldn't even have thanked him for it? It was true that on this particular occasion I was supposed to stay awake all night, but was there more to it?

At the end of the Second World War Phil's dad bought an old fishing schooner in Nova Scotia for a thousand dollars. Sixty feet long, of enormous beam, and gaff-rigged, the Bonne Pecheur was designed for rugged work in waters as unpredictable and dangerous as Lake Michigan. She was basically unsinkable, but she was not built for speed. Instead of slicing the water like a yacht, she plowed it like a trawler, so Mr. Azarian quickly lost interest in her.

By default, the boat became Phil's to do with as he pleased. His father trusted him like everybody else did, and he never seemed to care what Phil was up to. And Phil was up to a lot. He planned elaborately charted cruises up and down Lake Michigan with precise destinations and closely estimated sailing times. Phil never revealed much about these trips in advance but from the way he pored over the charts and studied the heavens through his sextant, none of us doubted he knew exactly where he was going and how. It took about five willing hands to sail the Bonne Pecheur, but sometimes as many as ten were aboard, all about Phil's age. The old schooner had neither radio nor engine but Phil's serious eye and Lake Michigan's abundant wind was all we thought we needed.

At sunset, when Phil brought me the coffee, we were about twelve hours out of Racine, our home port, headed toward the northern end of the lake, some three hundred miles away. He had made the coffee himself in the galley after asking me to take night watch at the helm. Well, he didn't exactly ask me. When someone wondered who had the night watch, he nodded in my direction. "The kid," he said. I wasn't sure whether it was an honor to be chosen to sail the schooner through the night or whether it was because everyone was too tired to volunteer and I was the youngest on board.

It had been a day of savage thunderstorms, the kind of day none of us would tell our parents about, and a day none of us would forget. It was an unwanted reminder that the Bonne Pecheur, or, as we called her, the Bony Pecker, was only sixty feet of boat in a lake fabled for storms that could sink ore freighters hundreds of feet long. The lake needed only ten seconds to remind us of this danger. The jib sheet broke free in the gale causing the jib, or forwardmost sail, to thrash wildly. Because the wind would quickly blow the sail to threads, and because it would be impossible to navigate without it, somebody had to go out onto the bowsprit to retrieve it. Ronnie Hansen got there before the rest of us. Just as he reached out for the lashing rope, the boat dove into a wave and Ronnie was gone. Not until then did any of us think it important that Ronnie was the only one on board who couldn't swim. He was lucky enough to have grabbed the rope and desperate enough to hold on until we somehow managed to pull him to the deck where he lay, gagging, coughing out water, and gasping for breath.

Finally, the storms passed, and as the sun set on a cloudless horizon we ate a few soggy sandwiches in silence. After Phil brought me the coffee, the others went to bed and the two of us watched the last traces of light leave the west. He told me that he wanted me to hold a course just above northnortheast, then turned on the light in the compass and pointed to a reading of about 10 degrees. He checked to see that all the running lights were working then disappeared into the cabin.

IT WAS SOON completely dark except for the compass and the running lights. A powerful, steady wind was blowing out of the west-northwest, an almost perfect wind direction for the bearing Phil had chosen. The temperature had dropped about twenty degrees and I pulled on the sweaters he had left for me.

The boat was riding huge swells the storm had raised and now pushed even higher by the freshening west wind. Since there was no level or steady place to rest the bottle, I had to hold it delicately with one hand while I gripped the wheel with the other. As soon as I became familiar with the rhythm of the schooner's surge and roll, I took the first tentative sips of coffee.

Standing in the cockpit of the Bony Pecker under the faultless heavens, I discovered the one adult privilege that did not taste bad, smell bad, or open a pained inwardness. As with everything else, Phil had his own way of making coffee—boiling it unfiltered in a large enamel pot with condensed milk, corn syrup, and egg shells—but, no matter, its essential muskiness was unmistakable and irresistible.

It was not only the taste. There was the sudden absence of fatigue, and then the clarity. Especially the clarity. The hiss and thunder of the boat's mastery of these great waves, the creaking of ropes in their hardwood blocks, the high moan of the wind in the sails and rigging, all this intensified and became more real than I was to myself. It is what I would later learn to call direct perception, the noninterference of a self-absorbed ego. Thoughts came and fled as lightly as the spray, emptying the mind but also enlarging it like the night sky now washed clean by its storms. Even the old schooner seemed to forget who she was, rising on this new air as much bird as boat.

Because there was no moon and because we were a hundred miles from the nearest city lights, the stars were as bright on the horizon as they were straight above. Suddenly the running lights and compass seemed artificial and unnecessary so I switched them off. The effect was astounding. With nothing now but starlight, the sails took on a mysterious glow as though they were lit from within and the rigging lifted its spidery profile into an ocean of galaxies. Now, without the compass, I could keep my course only by aiming the boat at planets and constellations. I held the top of the mainmast in the Corona Borealis, the bowsprit pointed at Venus, the foresail riding in Orion, and the Pleiades in command of the open sky to the west. The horizon was no longer the point where water met sky but the dome of stars that contained the whole known universe.

As promised in the arrival of the arctic high that created this storm in the first place, the wind held at fifteen to twenty knots through the night. It gradually moved to the north, however, and every half hour or so I would have to scramble about in the starlight setting the sails for a closer tack, making for a lively job at the helm. I finished the coffee in a couple of hours and tossed the empty bottle far out into the darkness, but its effects did not pass so quickly.

My thoughts raced, playing with the events of the day. I saw how different this night would have been if Ronnie had not had the luck to catch the jib sheet as the wave swept him off. In the clarity of recollection, I saw how Phil sprang to the helm when Ronnie disappeared and yelled at us over the wind that he was jibing, or turning away from the wind—the standard procedure for man overboard. But because the natural tendency of the boat in a high wind is to turn into the wind, a tendency made even stronger by the loss of the jib, he could not by himself overcome the resisting pressure of the rudder and his maneuver failed. And now, as the schooner ducked and surged in strong but somewhat lighter air, I realized with some shock that Phil had made an error that could have meant the loss of all of us. With the wind at fifty or sixty knots, the maneuver Phil attempted would almost certainly have blown the masts off the boat, perhaps capsizing her in the process. Why hadn't Phil thought of this? If it was clear to me, why had he not seen this danger? Did I know something he didn't?

The stars began to fade and I realized we had sailed into dawn. Within a half hour, a brilliant finger of sun lay on the rim of the lake. Suddenly Phil was standing there hugging himself in the cold morning air. I turned to tell him what a fine and uneventful night it had been when he stared at the sun and froze.

"What's the sun doing there?"

"It's coming up," I said cheerily.

He leapt over to the compass, looked at it in disbelief, and pointed back at the horizon. "No, what's it doing *there*?"

I turned to look at the sun myself.

"What have you been *doing*? Do you realize what *course* you're on?"

Just as I started to tell him that I didn't vary so much as a degree all night, that I never once lost our location in the stars, I understood what had happened.

Phil got his sextant from the cabin, aimed it at the horizon, and closed his eyes in silent calculation.

"My God, kid," he whispered in horror. "You're thirty miles off course! You realize how many hours we've lost?" He yelled into the cabin for someone to take the helm.

Still slightly under the spell of caffeine and starlight, I saw Phil's fury from something of a distance. Since it had not yet touched me, it was an entity in itself, light as air, fascinating to watch like a storm over someone else's horizon. It was at that moment that the mystical vision occurred.

IT WASN'T a vision in the sense that I actually beheld something. It was rather that I saw everything exactly as it was but also—not as it was. I remembered adjusting the course to the stars, lashing the wheel, scrambling forward along the narrow strip of deck between the cabin and the gunwales to adjust the sails and tighten down the sheets. Then what I saw was this: instead of the boat sailing off her course on a long arc across Lake Michigan, chasing the stars in their westward drift, it was the lake, the earth itself, turning away from the stars. The earth was rolling in her own sea but under us, not with us. As for the Bonne Pecheur, she held unerringly to her course through the galaxies.

Phil, the boat, the lake, the morning sun, noises of waking boys, all this was the same. Yet it was all different. I saw nothing extraordinary but everything I saw seemed extraordinary. It was a moment that came and went as weightlessly as everything else had that night. But as it went, it took with it the innocence of seeing in the old way.

The old way of seeing is strictly pre-Copernican but it has a fierce grip on our everyday consciousness. There we still dwell at the center of our world. Everything revolves around us. A straight line is not determined by the fixed positions of the sun and stars but by fixed positions on the moving earth. To the post-Copernican consciousness, this is not a straight line but an arc. The two ways of seeing are that of the ego and the soul. The ego is the fixed earth's agent in us; the soul is the heaven's. The ego is concerned with centers, the soul lives on margins, circumferences, horizons. Limitlessness is the natural element of the soul, a dread foe of the ego. When Pascal said he was terrified to see the small space he occupied "swallowed up in the infinite immensity of spaces of which I am ignorant and which know me not," he was speaking with the voice of the ego. It was the Pascal who was fighting to hold the center, even when he, better than anyone, knew the center was gone.

Mystical vision is the way the soul sees. It has no object. It does not occur because something unusual has come into view and demands to be looked at. The ego looks for something new within its field, while the field remains the same. The sails appeared ghostly to me and the stars brilliant but they were just sails and stars. There was no epiphany in that vision, no crack in the finite wall. At the age of fifteen, still innocent of religious ideas, I simply took what I got. Ten years later, full of ideas and full of the doubt they inevitably come with, I would have wanted the heavens to open, an un-mistakable sign to appear; better yet, a voice. The ego wants nothing less than to see God. The soul knows, however, that if the Divine were to appear, the ego would not recognize it. The heavens cannot open for the soul; they are already open.

This is why Bayazid, when he had a vision of flying through an atmosphere a million times larger than our own until he saw the field of Eternity and the Tree of Oneness, declared it all a cheat. It was an object, something "out there" in relation to which he was an amazed observer but an ob-server nonetheless. This was not vision but a vision, not a new way of seeing but something new to see. It is one thing to see something remarkable appearing inexplicably in the world, it is quite another to see the world itself as remarkable and all of existence as inexplicable.

The heavens that spread above the deck of the Bony Pecker that night were no different for me than they had al-ways been. If anything, they were vaster, colder, more empty of life than ever before. If this spinning madness of stars had a center, it could hardly be a soul, as Plato thought, but only a dumb-point, an indifferent conjunction of invisible geo-metric lines. Wherever it is that we dwell, it is certain only that nothing revolves around us; we are mere marginals wheeling pointlessly in our own sidereal eddy. The universe is just as the mystics say: its circumference is nowhere, its center is everywhere.

Marginalizing the ego, abandoning it to the circumfer-ence, is a way of entering the soul. In fact, it might be more accurate to say that marginalizing the ego is precisely the work of the soul. This is the work the mystics call "naughting" the ego. It was not the infinite spaces that terrified Pascal; it was the spacelessness of the self within. There is good reason for his terror: Pascal was a person in whom the soul was awake and the ego desperate to grab any line that would save it from being swallowed by the boundless.

MYSTICAL VISION never comes when you expect it. If you could consciously and explicitly prepare yourself for it, you would know what you were preparing yourself for and therefore would already have it. Such is the work of the ego. The soul, however, is constantly at work in quite another way. This is a work as unseen by us as the vision is unexpected. That we have been readied for vision by the soul is obvious only afterwards. Then we can only be surprised to know that what we thought was preparation was something else altogether. In fact, the true preparation for vision is nothing like what we would choose for preparation.

Indeed, the grander the vision, the more extensive—and the more surprising—our preparation has been. Through the whole course of our ordinary life, veils are dropping away but as long as we are looking from the perspective of ego we never notice. Typically, my preparation was in the form of an error; that is, the ego's error.

The mystical vision that resulted did not come while I was sailing the stars; it came later, in the full light of morning, when I knew the nature of my error. The nighttime experience had been preparation, to be sure, but only preparation. Was there rapture in this experience? Yes. I would have to describe my state that night as ecstatic. High on caffeine, clearheaded, unselfconscious, awake, solitary, I was outside myself. This was close to bliss, ananda, satori, nirvana, samadhi, but it was not yet vision. It was experience—what some might call mystical experience. But not vision, not mystical vision, anyway.

Mystical vision requires inversion. Since we cannot seek it, it can only be what we cannot and would not seek. We must be turned away, found in error, unable to account for ourselves. It can come after a blunder, a false turn, a rejected plea, a painful self-revelation, an irrecoverable loss. My little stupidity was hardly a matter of remorse or grief but it was just enough for the soul to expose its spacelessness. Unlike Pascal I experienced no terror in my vision, but for good reason: I had not yet acquired enough ego to defend against the soul. It was an ego so fragmentary that it did not know the true danger to itself. I was awake enough to know an inversion had occurred but it would be decades before I knew its significance.

AFTER RONNIE HANSEN had taken the helm, Phil announced that he would have to change his original plans and sail into Muskegon. Although we never knew what these original plans were, Muskegon was a major port for oil and ore freighters and about the least romantic harbor on the Michigan side of the lake. There was a lot of grumbling.

As soon as we passed into the busy harbor, around the middle of the day, talk of beer and girls changed the mood on board. Before permitting anyone to go ashore, Phil announced that we would set sail for Wisconsin about an hour before nightfall, in time to clear the harbor and its heavy commercial traffic before dark. Then he assigned each of us on-board orders. Mine was to clean the galley, and right away. The others could wait until they came back from shore.

Because the galley had not been cleaned since before the storm and because we had been making hamburgers in it all day, every utensil on board and every surface was coated with grease and ketchup. There was little chance I would get ashore at all. Without Phil saying it, I knew this duty was a kind of punishment for my starry ineptitude at the helm.

Soon the boat was empty and I dropped into the galley. It was several hours before I got to the pots and pans—the last part of my job. Making one last check of the cabin for food scraps and dirty dishes, I noticed in a cubby over Phil's bunk the crafted leather case that contained his sextant. We'd had a little instruction in the use of the sextant in sailing class but I never quite got the hang of it. Why not give it a shot right now, I suggested to myself.

I climbed to the deck and aimed the sextant at the horizon. But the horizon didn't appear. I turned the sextant around. Still nothing. I shook the instrument to see if there was something loose in it, but nothing rattled. When I tried to wipe the lenses with the dish towel hanging over my shoulder, I saw what was wrong. There was no lens in this instrument. The sextant didn't work.

Suddenly there was another inversion but this time it was most definitely not mystical. What came up was an utterly different vision of Phil. I recalled the way he would brace himself against the mast like some ancient sea captain, holding the sextant up against the sky, making long lists of numbers, then calculations, transcribing a series of numbers, arrows, and geometric figures to his maps, all the while asking for complete silence lest he make a serious navigational error. So Phil was a fake.

And now I realized I had never actually seen Phil write his name with both hands, nor did I notice that the Bony Pecker ever seemed to sail faster when he was at the helm. And then there was the question of his foolish and dangerous attempt to jibe when Ronnie had gone overboard.

A wild unmystical joy swept over me when I saw what I had on Phil. Instead of punishment, I now knew this galley assignment was Phil's undoing. Earlier when he brought me the cup of coffee I flattered myself with the thought that I was his equal, then he sent me to the galley as though reminding me I was after all his inferior, but now . . .

I returned to scrubbing the pans with high energy, eager for the return of the crew.

THEN IT HAPPENED again. Another inversion. This was true mystical vision. This I could never have anticipated. Another image of Phil appeared before me in the empty boat, totally different from all the others. I studied the seriousness in his face, the slightly worried expression, the distance in his eyes. He was a fake all right, but one I now understood. Phil *had* to be a fake. There was no other way of hiding the fact that his inner rigging was full of stars. What Phil was navigating no earthly sextant could measure. It was a voyage invisible, hidden from his friends, his father, even the school principal. But it was invisible in a way that I recognized. And now a new equality emerged. I doubted that Phil and I would ever travel on the same inner vessel but I knew that we were both marginals and both on the same galactic journey into the great void that contains us all. How about Ronnie and the others? Why would they be any less marginal? I was standing before a boundlessness that could swallow the stars in a heartbeat.

I didn't know it then, but after we secured the Bonne Pecheur to her own buoy at the end of that week and said our "So long, Phil" and "See ya, Kid" to each other, I would never see Phil again. He went away to college a few days later, Mr. Azarian sold the old schooner, and what happened to Phil I never knew.

But even if I had foreseen that, I would not have said anything to him about the sextant, much less about the stars. What, after all, does an adolescent have to say about galactic navigation? Besides, what I did was enough. Before I had finished the pans, I noticed a familiar enamel pot. I rescued a handful of eggshells from the garbage, poured out a cup of Karo syrup, added a cup of ground coffee, stirred in some water, and started boiling Phil a quart.

A Deeper Dreamer

Then even nothingness was not, nor existence.
   There was no air then, nor the heavens beyond it.
What covered it? Where was it? In whose keeping?
   Was there then cosmic water, in depths unfathomed?
Then there was neither death nor immortality,
   nor was there then the touch of night and day.
The One breathed windlessly and self-sustaining.
   There was that One then, and there was no other.
In the beginning desire descended upon it—
   that was the primal seed, born of the mind.
The sages who have searched their hearts with wisdom
   know that which is kin to that which is not.
But, after all, who knows, and who can say
   whence it all came, and how creation happened?
The gods themselves are later than creation,
   so who knows truly whence it has arisen?
Whence all creation had its origin,
   he, whether he fashioned it or whether he did not,
he who surveys it all from highest heaven,
   he knows—or maybe even he does not know.

RIG VEDA, X:129

I T HAPPENED while I was washing the dishes. It was dark outside, maybe ten o'clock, and the old house was sleeping in a huge quiet. Suddenly I was not alone. There was a presence to which I was present. It was nothing auspicious or alarming or even surprising, only a subtle existential shift as I became an other to an other. I stopped, stood back from the sink, and looked down.

There was a mouse on my sneaker.

She was a half-sized mouse, only a few weeks old, her body no bigger than her head, and obviously not yet wise in the ways of a mouse's world. Having discovered the treasure of seeds and pollen that had accumulated in the seams and laces of my shoe while I was mowing the lawn earlier in the day, it couldn't have mattered less to her that it was the shoe of a giant. I shifted my foot about an inch to see what would happen. Nothing. I softly stamped on the floor. Nothing. I took a full step and gently waved my foot. She just hung on and stayed at her business. There was no interfering with this meal. Then I thought of Charlie the cat.

"Look, sweetie," I said, leaning down, "there's a whole out-of-doors full of this stuff and if you insist on being this careless you may become a meal yourself." I explained that although Charlie was probably upstairs asleep, he could appear as suddenly and silently as she had. These warnings made no impression so I returned to my work in the sink while she continued at hers. She paused only briefly to race from one shoe to the other.

A few minutes later, when the last plate had been put away, we arrived at a critical moment. I was insistent on reading but she was by no means finished with her nibbling. So I headed into the living room in slow loping steps to indicate that dinner was over. She slipped off the toe of the shoe but managed to catch the end of a lace. This made a wild ride of it but we reached the living room with the dilemma unresolved.

Since Charlie was sure to come downstairs to investigate the unlikely tone of this conversation, I decided on a bolder action. Lifting her from the shoe, I explained that although I cared for her health, I cared more for her safety and for that reason she was going out to the lawn where this bounty had originated. Because I had expected her to dart, I had seized her firmly, wrapping her entirely in my hand. But she lay in this grip like it was the womb from which she had so recently emerged. I could feel the racing of her diminutive heart but otherwise not a twitch

Holding her up where I could get a good view of her face, I studied it for signs of fear or panic and saw none. I saw signs of nothing else either. This was not a face to be read or interpreted. In a way, it was not even a face. All the parts were there but there was no telling who or what was looking through them. The black lidless dots that were her eyes must have been taking in every detail of my enormous visage but it was a vision uncompromised by the merest flicker of reflection or emotion. No epistemological subtleties here.

Was someone looking at me or was it just that I was being seen? What was I cupping in my hand, some artifice of nature as efficient and empty as a computer chip, or another being residing in a mysterious nonspace behind those expressionless eyes? Only this seemed certain: I was a reality to her, another being, in a way I can be for no machine. On a larger question, I had no clue at all: was she, to any degree whatsoever, a reality for herself?

The best we can do, I think, is to settle for something in between. She sees but she does not see that she sees—as in a dream, but a dream from which she cannot awake. So, what is the difference between us? I can wake from my dreams. But do I wake completely? Do I, too, dream a reality that is no more than fragments of reality to a deeper consciousness?

The Hindus speak of four levels of consciousness. Contrary to the usual view, they consider the waking state of the day world the most superficial and partial level of awareness. Dreaming sleep is the next level. Below that is the consciousness of dreamless sleep. Ordinarily we would consider this a loss of consciousness but the Hindus see here a deeper wakefulness hidden from both the waking I and the dreaming I. The purest consciousness lies still deeper. It is that which is aware of the other states and aware of itself at the same time. Because it is perfectly self-aware and needs nothing else to be itself, this is our true self.

The simplest evidence we have for the existence of this pure self-consciousness is that in waking from dreamless sleep or even from a dream we are always certain we are the same person who went to sleep. There is a continuity of identity that remains constant through all states of consciousness, however weird or extreme. We may not know exactly who or what we are but we never think we have become someone else.

The mystical relevance of this analysis of consciousness is that while this deepest state is not directly known to the other levels of consciousness, each of those levels is perfectly known to it. In other words, self-knowledge is not knowing who or what the true self is; it is being known by that self. To enter into ourselves is therefore increasingly to discover how well we are already known to ourselves.

When my friend Bill said you can't be a philosopher without a cat, I was reminded of the silence we share with animals, the silence that precedes all speech and makes speech possible. Staring into the unblinking eyes of this half-sized mouse, it was not the mystery of language that held my attention but the question of our deepest identity and the surprising way we are known to ourselves. If I have something in common with Charlie, do I have something in common with this simpler yet more distant being? Each of us remains permanently ignorant of whatever the other knows. Our separate knowledges will never wake to each other. But is there a hidden way she is known that parallels the way I am known to my true self? Is there a still deeper self that knows us both?

A subtle restlessness in her tiny body alerted me to the responsibility I had taken for her well-being. As I carried her out to the yard, I explained that although she takes risks with giants, the night hunters are another matter, especially the great horned owl that presides over the lawn and garden and the hill behind the house. I know, since for years I have been finding little balls of mouse-hide and bone beneath the owl's favorite trees. The pleading was all in vain because when she discovered that the grass was a feast of its own, she was about as concerned with my alarms as with the surprising chill that was sliding down the hill and across the lawn. A June frost? I went in to build a fire.

NO MATTER how bizarre or terrifying a dream may be, the reality of it to the dreamer, or the dreaming I, is not in question. Only when we wake from it does the dream seem strange. It is strange because it does not fit into waking reality. We are then faced with a decision: either we reconcile the dream with the day world by interpreting it or we forget it.

This way the dream becomes the property of the waking I, and the deeper consciousness that was at work in it goes back into hiding.

The usual way of interpreting a dream is to translate its content into terms familiar to the waking I. If we followed the Hindus' insight into levels of consciousness, we would reverse this process. We would ask ourselves what the dreaming I knows about the waking I that the waking I cannot know about itself. The mystic's concern here is to know how I am already known to my deeper, truer self.

Waking from a dream, therefore, is not returning to reality so much as it is coming into a more partial vision of reality. From the perspective of the deeper consciousness, day-world wakefulness is a form of spiritual sleep.

But it is a restless sleep. The day world has its own weirdness. Strange as the dream may seem to the waking I, the waking I never attains the certainty about the day world the dreaming I had about the dream world. In the dream things are what they are but the day world is always something other than what it is. The shock of waking is the shock of confronting an actuality we cannot think away but an actuality that demands interpretation. Full clarity, morning light, the absence of shadows are not enough. If when we awake from the dream we find it does not fit into reality, when we enter the waking world we find that reality does not fit into reality.

Freud thought the purpose of the dream was to keep the sleeper from waking. If we dream when we are asleep, we also dream to stay asleep. Can it be that the reverse happens in the day world, that we interpret to return to sleep—in this case, not to the deeper consciousness of the Hindus but to a waking sleep, as in a daydream? If so, we begin to glaze over just where our certainty about the world begins. When Freud surveyed the scientific view of reality he had inherited, he saw it as a kind of intellectual somnolence. It was an interpretation that forgot it was an interpretation. For Freud reality was nothing if not enigmatic. Things are never what they seem to the waking I. Even such everyday occurrences as slips of the tongue are full of hidden meanings.

The irony is that instead of listening to the restlessness that led Freud to his multiple interpretations of the waking world, we have been daydreaming many of his tentatively offered ideas—such as the mechanism of repression, the unconscious, the death instinct—as though they were unambiguous descriptions of reality. But the restlessness is more revealing. Freud's inability to settle on any one of his interpretations of the waking world hints he knew there was a deeper knowledge the day world would never recognize. No wonder scholars have often pointed to the influence of the mystics on Freud.

"Philosophy," Aristotle said, "begins in wonder." This is the remark of a waking thinker who like Freud found himself challenged by the enigmas of the real world. Aristotle was the heir of knowledges he knew he had to wake from. Things are not made of what we think, Thales declared in the morning century of Greek thought, they are made of water. As if this were not implausible enough, Heraclitus denied there were any things at all; instead there is just motion and change—not things that change, just change. Parmenides taught that if we see the many without seeing the One, we see nothing at all. Do not trust your senses, Plato warned, their very accuracy will lead you to falsehood; the Real is that which is invisible to the eye but visible to the awakened mind.

At the waking hour of Indian thought, the anonymous author of the tenth book of the Rig Veda, arguably the world's oldest piece of reflective writing, reasoned that because there is being, there must be something from which it originates. But this can't be another being for the problem of origin would continue. Who could know how all this came about? Only the gods. But perhaps the gods are still daydreaming and don't know this either. In that very first awakening to wakefulness, there is a distinct alarm that we might use thought to lead us from the wisdom that still hides in a deeper consciousness.

IN MODERN thought the awareness that there is something out there that we are not yet awake enough to see is the engine that drives the investigative mind. Relentless and systematic questioning: this is the spirit of scientific intelligence. In this spirit we dissect to see what connects, we dismember to understand the whole, we kill to catch life in its act.

The hope is that we will at some moment awake to precisely what is before us. We reassure ourselves that there must be a bottom to it all, an irreducible stuff out of which the universe is made or a discoverable set of laws to which the Heraclitean flux is faultlessly obedient. "Now we see in a glass darkly," Paul said, "then face-to-face." The investigative mind shares this eschatological fantasy. When we do get to the bottom, not a symbol will remain. All need for interpretation will have passed. What now seems extraordinary will then be simply ordinary. We will gaze at the face of the real as innocent with wonder as a field mouse.

However, this hope, that we will one day see what is there precisely as it is there, is being challenged at the same time that it is growing. And the challenge is coming from those who have most vigorously encouraged the quest to behold the real face to face. The reason is that the closer we get to the real the stranger it becomes, more and more unlike what we expected it to be. The most hardminded researchers into subatomic reality, for example, find themselves drawn into wild speculations about what is really there. We thought they would find a primal dust, a swarm of lifeless and identical realities, the atoms of Epicurus only smaller, that are the building units of all larger, composite beings. But in fact they are describing things more dreamlike than real, more made of empty space than substance. Far from relieving us of all need for interpretation, the need for it has grown. In fact, each attempt to end an interpretation calls for a new and more imaginative interpretation. If philosophy begins in wonder it also ends in wonder.

Although the modern scientific quest reveals levels of reality that reach beyond the limits of all existing knowledge, it is not yet the mystics' insight that we are known more deeply than we know. The restlessness that drives this quest, however, is a step toward the mystical because it derives from the awareness that the day world knowledge of the waking I is not to be trusted.

This awareness is intensified when it is seen that once interpretation enters, an interpreter enters with it. With all wonder there is a wonderer. No longer can we separate the reality we are looking at from the reality of the looking. What we see depends partly on what is there and partly on who is looking. This is the hermeneutical circle: all seeing is interpreting, all interpreting is the act of the interpreter; therefore, every interpreter must include the act of interpretation in what is being interpreted. For that reason, interpretation never comes to an end. Each new reading of reality carries the seeds of its own contradiction, requiring a still newer reading.

This could be one of the most disturbing elements in the modern quest for knowledge, disturbing because it wakes us from a daydreamer's certainty to a dawning limitlessness both without and within. It is the contemporary version of Pascal's terror: a physical reality so vast and a psychic reality so bottomless no place remains for a fixed ego. Yet it is just that insight that puts us at the threshold of a different vision. If philosophy begins and ends in wonder, so does the philosopher.

SUDDENLY I REALIZED that the book had lain unopened on my lap for an hour or more. The fire had long since ceased raging and I could feel the cold at my shoulder. There was a tiny sensation. Something had touched my shoe. Without even looking, I knew who it was. She was back.

Can this be the same mouse? I had shut and locked the door. As far as I knew, there wasn't a single open passage into the house. But that just told me how much I knew. What she knew of the house, I couldn't imagine. For more than two centuries she and countless generations of her ancestors had sped the interior passages of this house, like dreams racing through an unlit cerebral mass, without a design, with no light of their own, without an idea that this was even a house.

She quickly worked the lode on my sneakers and socks to the point of sufficient yield and started scouting out larger circles on the carpet and under the furniture. I finally got to my book, forgot the mouse, and let the fire burn out. Midnight came and went and the cool damp in the walls had absorbed whatever warmth had radiated from the fireplace. I went to bed.

As I pulled the featherbed over me and waited for the warmth to collect, I had a vision of the creature civilizations gathered around me in the old house: ants, spiders, moths, mealy worms, the phoebes that nest on the porch, swifts in the chimney, swallows in the eaves, silverfish, wood borers, newts, the red squirrels that collect their winter stores and pursue each other in frantic races through the rear attic, mosquitoes, gnats, lacewings, slugs, centipedes, pill bugs, milk snakes I have seen mating as they hang from a rafter in the basement, bats in the eaves and behind the shutters, caterpillars, the woodchucks who have built a huge mound of a house in the crawl space under the porch, earthworms, grubs, wasps, fat winter flies. The old house dreaming a thousand wordless knowledges, each eternally asleep to the others. . . .

MY BROTHER announced in the severest tone that I could no longer play golf with him. "You just don't play well enough for me," he said. As he spoke, I noticed he was packing his new clubs into the trunk of his car. The light flashed off the clubs and I saw what they were: the most famous brand one could possibly possess, magical instruments without which one could never be much of a golfer. I reached toward the bag. I just wanted to swing one, nothing more. He stood in my way so I couldn't touch them.

"Where are you going?" I asked.

"Dubuque," he said.

I moved closer, hoping he would notice and offer to take me with him. When he saw what I wanted, he laughed and said with scorn that the only way I could go along was to play as well as he.

"But, you know what? You'll never play well enough to get to Dubuque."

As he turned to leave, I took hold of his shoulders, begging him not to go, and woke up.

After the several seconds it required to be certain this was a dream, I was astonished to find that my face was wet with tears. It was not the tears that astonished but the fact that I had not been crying in the dream. These were the tears of another I, of an awakened I. Who is that I? And who is the I of the dream?

First, I went to work on the dream itself. Dubuque. I've never been to Dubuque, I know no one there and know nothing whatsoever about it except that it is in Iowa and therefore near the center of the continent. So here's a clue: going to Dubuque is going to the center.

What else? As far as I knew, my brother had had no connection with Dubuque either. So why would he go there? At least the golfing part of the dream was less mysterious. As boys we spent numberless hours whacking balls around golf courses all over our corner of the state, often with our father. Because I was older, I regularly beat my brother and in time could hold my own with my father. I grew tired of the game after I left home but my brother continued to play with growing intensity into adulthood, until his premature and sudden death a year or so before I had this dream. Golf had become so important to his life that we decided to spread his ashes across his favorite course.

As my brother left for Dubuque, I knew in the dream that he would never come back. The dreaming I, however, did not see this as death. Or maybe it was that death had a very different meaning to the dreaming I than to the waking I. My waking I sees death as a place of no return, a terminus, a darkened nonspace where nothing ever happens. My anguish as the dreaming I was not that I would lose my brother to death but that my brother would leave me behind. This was the highest achievement of my brother's life; Dubuque was the treasured goal for every golfer, open only to the masters of the sport. Because he was leaving me behind, it was I who was dying.

Then I noticed that death and Dubuque begin with the same letter. So does my brother's name: David. In fact, the word Dubuque pronounces the initials of his name: D.B.C. A journey into the center, into death, into his own center, a journey that left me outside knowing I could never get there because I lacked the skill and I lacked the magical instruments he would not even let me touch.

The narrative core of the dream is a conflict between two wills. My brother's resolve to head off for Dubuque was as absolute as my desire to go with him. It was a struggle to the death. This time the younger was the superior competitor. And he knew it. What I knew was that he clearly intended to win a match with his big brother that he could never lose again.

This interpretation came without too much difficulty. In fact, I wanted to leave it with that and forget the dream. But there was the issue of the tears. Something wanted to wake me from this interpretation. The dreaming I knew something about myself the waking I did not want to know.

The dreaming I was not crying. I was crying, but which I was this? Could there be a watcher who was not asleep and knew the deeper story of the dream? At last, I saw the obvious: this dream did not happen to me. I, as the deeper knower, dreamed it. I was putting it on for myself. I was trying to get my attention from a deeper level of wakefulness, to wake myself from a resistant somnolence. My brother did not inform me of anything; I knew all this already.

The issue here is not whether I will wake from the dream but whether I will wake to a still deeper I: the true dreamer of the dream. I can find a meaning for this dream by one or another interpretation, but can I find in myself the dreamer who knows exactly what the dream is about? Who also knows what the waking I is about.

In other words, the desire to find an interpretation for this dream is a trick to keep me from seeing that although I have awakened there is a still deeper wakefulness. So I must try not to fall for the trick by contenting myself with speculation about its symbols and hidden meanings. This dream does not hide what I don't know but what I do know. And what I do know is the most obvious truth of all, as obvious to me now as to the boy I was then.

I knew that as I came in round after round with better golf scores, my brother was suffering a secret crisis. I was careful never to gloat over my superiority; I was even generous in victory. But this generosity was itself part of a strategy to create a dilemma for my brother and to keep him in it. I knew from our earliest years together this was a child who wanted so desperately to triumph at any game we played that he would die to win. The strategy at which I had become such a master was to make sure that he would keep losing by reinforcing in him the self whose single passion was to defeat his older brother. But, of course, the real point of this strategy was to brace up a false self of my own. Only if David stayed in the game could I remain the winner I needed to be. If he refused to play, or took his play elsewhere as he did in the dream, this carefully arranged self would have no way to continue. The story of the dream is this self fighting for its life.

So the self with which I was in such lethal struggle was not my brother's but my own. When I seized my brother by the shoulders, I was not begging him to forgive me for what I had done to him in our youth, I was begging him to help me in what I cannot do myself. I wanted him to take me with him. The terror I experienced as the dreaming I was not his death but the awareness that I could not achieve such a death by myself.

FOR A PERIOD of five years my brother and I fell out of touch. We called each other a few times but never even talked about getting together. Neither of us understood why the events in our lives at the time had so distracted us. When we did finally meet, we saw at once how much we had needed each other in those years. The reunion was surprisingly emotional, hugging and kissing each other like lost children.

It was a phone call from my brother that started it. He wanted me to meet his new wife. We made elaborate plans. Of course, it included golf. I got out my old clubs, cleaned them of last year's dirt, and flew out to meet him.

It was a cool November morning. The course was all but empty. When my brother set his clubs in the golf cart, I noticed for the first time that they were the famous brand used now by most of the pros, widely discussed in the sports magazines. Even their cost was famous. When he saw me admiring them he tossed a seven iron at me. "Here," he said, "see what you think." Maybe technology can make real advances, I thought to myself as I swung the club, amazed by the magical feel of it in my hands.

"You hit first," Dave said. I was a little nervous as I teed up the ball, and wondered why. He knew I had hardly played all these years so I had an excuse for playing badly. It was not a fifty-four-year-old man, however, but a fifteen-year-old boy leaning over the ball adjusting the tee to a perfect height for the driver. The ball shot off with exciting speed and then, as though hit by a second golfer, it right-angled sharply off into the woods.

Dave said nothing. He lightly pulled the priceless driver from the golf bag and brushed a spot of dust from it. I think I began seeing what had happened to him when he teed his ball. It was a soft, almost balletic action. He leaned forward on one leg, the other balanced out behind, placed the ball delicately on the tee without adjusting it, and stood back in his position—all in one seamless move. There was a still center here, all right. He studied the top of the club for a moment, placed it behind the ball, and started his backswing. Then I knew for sure.

In the weeks afterward, reflecting on this moment, I had to admit to myself that the panic I felt as the club started back had to do with loss. First, I thought Dave was going to lose the club. He seemed to have nothing to do with it. It was attached to nothing. It would simply drop to the ground. Then I thought he had lost his swing, that he would never finish it. There was such indifference here that hitting the ball was the last thing he had on his mind; he would get to the top of the backswing and just forget. Finally, I knew what it was. I had lost my brother. He had become someone else.

His ball did not start like mine. Mine was ballistic, it couldn't wait to blow out of there. In fact, his didn't start at all; it was merely the swing continued. It left in the easy, who-gives-a-damn way in which Dave had walked onto the tee to begin with. You could tell as it lifted itself with an energy of its own that there was only one golfer behind this stroke. The ball hung there for a while, barely visible against the gray November sky, musing, taking its time. When it was ready, it dropped softly to the center of the fairway, miles away.

"Could you see what I did wrong?" I asked him.

"Sure."

"Have any ideas how I might improve my swing?"

Dave smiled. He understood what I was asking.

Before we got to the green on the first hole, he had started on my grip. As we went along, he took my whole swing apart, element by element. He would lecture briefly on the philosophy of such matters as placing the right elbow, finding the proper plane for the swing as a whole, finishing out the follow-through.

Not until the second round did he get to the real issue. After I had knocked still another drive into the woods, he said, "You know what you've got to do. You've got to get my father out of your swing."

His expression "my father," a habit of speech from childhood, gave his words an oddly vulnerable quality. That was certainly part of the reason his remark hit me with such force. The remark also explained why I felt I had lost him. The liberation I saw in his golf swing was about as available to me as the Buddha's. Since he had traveled this route himself, he was well acquainted with its terrible paradoxes. He could give me years of philosophy on the golf swing without repeating himself, making sure I became an expert on every detail. But that's the easy part. The hard part is not picking this up, but dropping something else. I think that's why he spoke in this most intimate of childhood voices.

During the time of my early childhood my father had been a professional boxer. He was by instinct a slugger. He obviously believed if he could get his full power into a single blow he could do it all. As with much else in life, he didn't hit a golf ball, he pulverized it. Of course, this was terrifying; it was also thrilling. But I think my brother saw the danger in it before I did.

A chill mist slowly settled on the course and before the day was out it became a fine rain. We played 45 holes altogether, two and a half rounds, stopping only when it had become too dark to continue. Standing on the last hole, staring down at the lights in the clubhouse, there was no chance we would see where our balls landed. But by now, I knew the course well enough to know about where the green lay, slightly downhill, about 340 yards away, heavily banked with sand traps. I had played about half a dozen holes perfectly but none of them in sequence so I knew I still had a long way to go. At least I thought I knew what that way was. A small edge of confidence had developed.

"You hit first," Dave said just like on the first hole, then added, "Hit the shit out of it."

For a joyous second I let my whole youth have its turn and I did. I hit the shit out of it. The ball disappeared into the dark. Dave stepped up. I could see the added power in his swing but just barely. He didn't even bother watching the ball.

"Where do you think mine went?" I asked.

"Gone."

"How about yours?"

"Home."

WHO, THEN, was weeping in the dream, and why? The dreaming I who felt the terror was not the I who wept. The tears were not from the terror of being left behind. There must be a sadness here much deeper than fear. I could not have dreamed this dream if I had not known all along that what my brother really wanted was not to beat me at golf but to win me to himself. It is the I who understood this who wept; the sadness was that I would not let myself be loved. This is what I knew about myself I did not want to know.

After the funeral, I was walking across the parking lot with my brother's son Brad, when he suddenly took me by the arm, walked to his father's car, and opened the trunk. "I know Dad would want you to have these," Brad said. The magical instruments. They now wait for me in the closet next to the fireplace. I use them a few times a year, but not very well. But it doesn't matter. The magic in them works anyway.

HAVE I EXHAUSTED the interpretive challenge of the dream and returned myself to the clarity of the dreamer? Have I awakened to all its truths? Not at all. The deeper dreamer, the fully awake self that I most truly am, still has knowledges so hidden I do not yet know what I know.

The next time I was in the country, my son Jamie volunteered to make the fire. "Dad, look at this," he said as he shoveled out the ashes. "It must have got stuck behind the screen." He slid the body of the mouse onto the carpet with the edge of his shoe.

I picked her up. No need for a womblike grip now. Her face seemed sucked back into her skull. I couldn't even tell where her eyes had been. For such a tiny corpse, such an enormous emptiness. "Who were you?" I whispered.

Vision in a Deathwrap

There is no life in thee, now, except that rocking life imparted by a gentle rolling ship; by her, borrowed from the sea; by the sea, from the inscrutable tides of God. But while this sleep, this dream is on ye, move your foot or hand an inch; slip your hold at all; and your identity comes back in horror. Over Descartian vortices you hover. And perhaps, at mid-day, in the fairest weather, with one half-throttled shriek you drop through that transparent air into the summer sea, no more to rise for ever. Heed it well, ye Pantheists!

HERMAN MELVILLE,
ON RIDING THE CROW'S NEST OF A WHALING SHIP

WHEN I WAS LIVING in a student dormitory with my family as its professor-in-residence, I decided at a late hour to accept an invitation to the students' annual Halloween blowout. This was not an easy decision. The year was 1969. The dormitory was in Greenwich Village. It was a time and place in which Halloween seemed to last all year. To rise above the standard level of costuming for a special event placed a high tax on the imagination.

I decided to attend when my children supplied the requisite inspiration. Their reasoning was simple. I was then teaching a popular course on death and dying. "So, go as a mummy." I stripped to my undies and in less than an hour they had wrapped me with rolls of toilet paper and Scotch tape until they achieved what they thought was a genuine Egyptian model of the genre. Limited to what vision was available through a narrow slit over one eye, I made my way stiffly to the elevator, where one of the children pressed the button.

When the door opened on the floor where the party was now in full swing, the effect was everything I could have anticipated, and more. An already animated crowd met my appearance with a full sixties eruption. I had feared that they would quickly guess that this was just Carse done up as death but, no doubt about it, I knew at once I was quite an anonymous mummy. I passed through the mob with the genuine thrill of watching them light up in theatrical horror.

In a few minutes I had exhausted the initial impact of my entrance and took my place in the crowd as new monsters slunk and leapt from the elevator. By the time the party had found its own level of dancing and whooping, the novelty of my costume had been spent and I was being ignored. So I lurched about more like a zombie than a mummy, pressing my single eye against the masks of other freaks. It was then that I first had the feeling not a single person was looking back at me. They quickly took in my costume, reacted appropriately, and turned somewhere to get a reaction to their own display. Suddenly I was a bore and my larger effort to get attention made me a larger bore. Despite the relentless artillery of ear-numbing music and the general zany happiness of some two hundred adolescents, there was a chilling silence inside my deathwrap of toilet paper. No one was looking at me.

It was all meant as a joke, I reassured myself. I came to act dead, not to be treated as dead. But the joke had lost its joker and what I experienced for a few truly terrifying moments was not loneliness or rejection but nonexistence. Not seen, not heard, unable to get attention, I felt the substance of my selfhood whiting out.

I HAD DISTINCTLY sensed that no one was looking at me. However, in recollection, I realized that the other freaks had actually looked into the slit over my eye. In fact, the slit may have been the costume's most effective element. It was genuinely hideous: a featureless face containing nothing but an eyeball. And that's what they were looking at: the eyeball. The electricity of their reaction is perfectly intelligible: they saw no one looking; they only saw themselves being looked at. That was enough. They could safely return to their gorillas, headless princesses, scarfaces, and drooling geeks, leaving me to cope on my own with the awful awareness that it is not the eyeball that sees.

I knew, of course, I could take the costume off at any moment and everyone in the place would immediately know who I was. In fact, they would greet my foolery with laughter and applause. But the panic had a deeper purchase. There was something here I was already familiar with. I had been in this deathwrap before; in fact, I was in it even as I got into it. "Carse!" I could imagine them howling. "Yo, Carse, great costume, man." They would know me all right. But as what?

Carse is an identity for both them and me within a complicated but very specific web of predictable actions and reactions. They and I had already been at work establishing our
identities at an earlier, much larger party, the one we were all
throwing when this one started. I came wrapped for that one
as well and there, too, we duck and bob with each other,
maintain our distances, taking care not to touch. This is the
big show we call the university.

Sufis speak of their *nafs*, or the false self that takes the
place of the soul. Somewhat more complicated than the concept of the ego, the *nafs* refers to all that in ourselves which
has become an object for others or for ourselves. It is our visible self, the tangible, public aspect of a personality. It is what
we see when we look at ourselves, it is what we present to
others to be seen by them. It is what stands in the way of our
oneness with others, with ourselves, with the Divine. The
nafs in each of us has a life of its own, logical, powerful, real.
Sometimes the Sufis describe it as a hungry yellow dog that
stays begging at our side until we learn to drive it away.
Sometimes it pops out of our throats in the form of a mouse
or a young fox.

When the spooks looked at my eyeball, it was enough for
them to know they were being seen. They knew their *nafs*
was visible to the person looking through this eye. But since
they did not see me looking back out at them, I had become
invisible to them—and also to myself. The defining lines of
my identity had gone slack and I felt my very being slipping
through them. I wanted to tear back the costume just enough
that they could see that it was me, Carse, their professor. The
panic came not because I was hidden behind the mummy but

because I would have been invisible even as they recognized me. The identity I present to the world is a self to be seen and not the self who sees. But this is the identity I present to myself as well. Carse is my *nafs*.

SOMEWHERE AROUND this time a friend in the law school asked me if I could play the role of a policeman in a moot court trial. After I agreed, I saw why, of all people, he wanted me to do it. He had been able to borrow a uniform from a cousin who worked as a cop in a suburban community. His cousin was just my size.

I hadn't gone fifty yards from my apartment in my policeman's suit when a car stopped to ask for directions. There was something odd in the way the driver spoke to me. She did not start by saying "Excuse me." She just asked how she was supposed to get there from here. She seemed to assume I had nothing else to do but give her directions. Before the end of the block, I noticed two young men abruptly cross the street before I got close. After several people greeted me with an exceptionally friendly "Hello, officer," I began to observe how frequently people looked then looked away as though I weren't there at all. By the time I reached the park, I couldn't tell whether certain people were trying to make themselves invisible in the crowd or whether I had expected them to and therefore actually saw them do it. Before I reached the law school, I was not only used to being looked at as a cop, I was starting to see the world as a cop. In less than five city blocks.

When I entered the student courtroom, I got a number of approving looks for the fit of the uniform. Yes, I was perfect for the part, they seemed to be thinking. At once, the uniform became a costume and all traces of self-consciousness evaporated. Once the trial started, I slipped easily into the role of "cop." In fact, I forgot I was playing a role and even forgot what had happened an hour before on the street.

As I got back to the street and started home, however, I was sharply conscious of the difference between playing cop and being cop. On the stage, I could forget it was a role. On the street, it was not so simple. In fact, I tried distinctly not to play the role and just walk home. Still, there was no ignoring the fact that as I passed by the slightly ominous young men who sell drugs in the park, they quickly took their hands out of their pockets and talked to each other with exaggerated gestures and laughter as though they do nothing else all day. Even intending not to be a cop, I was passing through the world of a police officer. No matter what role I intended to play, the world was performing me as it saw me. Naturally, I did not have to accept this role but I couldn't ignore it either; I had to make an inner, focused effort not to be what I read myself to be in the eyes of the anonymous audience a city street had instantly become.

When I got home, I didn't take the uniform off, I threw it off. It was a palpable relief to get back into normal clothes: sneakers, jeans, and my worn Harris tweed sportcoat. In an hour or so I was on the street again, walking through the world as I know it, only slightly aware that I was not aware I was walking through the world of a college professor.

The mysticism of this five-block stroll begins to appear in the simple fact that I went from one fixed and solid world to another. On reflection, what appeared remarkable in this unremarkable event is that in passing so easily from world to world I did not experience the insubstantiality of these several worlds. This was no dumb show of illusory stage settings. On the contrary, each world presented itself as complete, in need of no further definition. Where is the mysticism here? Each world is the world of my *nafs*.

The Sufis are right, the *nafs* has an existence of its own. I cannot decide to have this or that *nafs*. It comes to me by itself. I certainly didn't whistle up the big yellow dog that walked those five blocks with me. It showed up by itself and knew perfectly well I would keep it fed. This *nafs* was the way I saw the world but it was also the way the world saw me. In fact, there is no difference here between seeing and being seen. I could not have seen the world as a cop until I was seen as one. How you see me shapes the world I live in. Indeed, the shape of that world comes from no other source. If you start seeing me as your hero, I will start seeing you as someone who needs the protection only I can give; see me as your enemy, I will quickly find grounds to oppose you. I would so like to think that the world I live in as a college professor is the world, period. But the world I know as a college professor is only the world that knows and is known by my *nafs*; therefore, it is a world known by someone I most certainly am not.

IN HIS SMALL classic, *The Vision of God*, Nicholas of Cusa puts the curious phenomenon of seeing through a characteristic mystical inversion. Since we can only be as we are seen, whoever looks at us plays a part in creating us and the world we live in. Nicholas reasons from this fact that God, the

Maker of all things, not only creates by vision but exists as vision: "I exist in that measure in which Thou art with me, and, since Thy look is Thy being, I am because Thou dost look at me, and if Thou didst turn Thy glance from me I should cease to be." If we look at God, therefore, we do not see another being out there existing independently of us; we see ourselves being seen. But, of course, we cannot see the seer through the face. We cannot see the face of God. Instead we see a multitude of faces around us, earthly faces, in each of which is a hidden seer. "In all faces is seen the Face of faces, veiled, enigmatic; even unveiled it is not seen, until above all faces we enter into a certain secret and mystic silence where there is no knowledge or concept of a face."

To the degree that every glance at us participates in the creation of our world, every glance participates in God's vision of us. No glance contains the whole of God's vision of us for God's vision has no limitations within itself. When we look into the eye of another for the eye of God, we see nothing resembling the Divine. "Thy face cannot be found except veiled; but that very darkness revealeth Thy face to be there, beyond all veils." In the eye of the other we see nothing looking at us; that nothing is the veiled eye of God.

It follows that our own seeing participates in the vision of God quite as much as any other. The vision of God, therefore, is not our vision *of* God but God's own vision by which all things are created. To the degree that we see anything at all, we see with the eye of God.

Nicholas, like most mystics, makes no distinction between seeing and knowing. Eckhart, writing a century earlier, offers another dimension of the relation of the seer to the seen, or the knower to the known. "God," he said, "does not 'know' this or that." Eckhart's odd remark says as much about knowledge as it does about God. The simpler half has to do with God. God is One. Not one of several, not the first of many. One. There is no other to this One, nothing which can be an object to it. To know this or that can only mean that in addition to God there is at least a this and a that.

As for the harder part, knowledge, we can know only that which is other, separate from us. All knowledge is knowledge of. There can be no knowledge except where the knower is distinct from the object of knowledge. Knowledge, therefore, is a recognition of our otherness to an other, it is itself evidence of our separateness. "When the soul knows something," Plotinus said, "it loses its unity."

On the other hand, the basic impulse of knowledge is to draw closer to the other, to make the strange familiar. When I was dressed as a cop and the two young men crossed the street ahead of me, I noticed. This was not just something I happened to see; it fed the appetite of an awakened intelligence. It was a strange fact I made familiar by seeing it as a phenomenon of my policeman world. There was a desire at work in this seeing. I wanted to join with other seers in it, enlarging it, thus stretching the boundary of my sight in the direction of the boundless.

The mysticism of our seeing and knowing is precisely what our *nafs* tries to hide from us. Our *nafs* wants its worlds to stay fixed, opaque, hostile to deeper vision. At the same time, and paradoxically, the *nafs* is a creation of our mystical longing for oneness—or as we usually experience it, familiarity. Knowing the world confirms our otherness to the world but it also reveals our desire to see what lies beyond its edges. It is an act of drawing closer not to the world but to other knowers.

By the time I had walked my five blocks I did not love the world I saw any more than I loved my own, probably less, but I did find that I had grown closer to policemen—and I don't even know any policemen. I had begun to see the world as they see it; they and I had begun to see it together. It was a step in the direction of the infinite.

I know of a gifted young anthropologist who went to live in an isolated culture in the South Pacific. When one of her friends learned she was returning to the United States for the first time in over ten years, she was invited to speak at her old college. Though reluctant, she accepted. During her talk, the audience, mostly anthropologists and anthropology students, became increasingly disturbed by the way she confused the words "they" and "we." They saw that she was not talking *about* these people but as one of them. She had "gone out" to this culture as an observer of it but her colleagues soon found her instead to be a native of it who had come to observe them. They expressed their dismay at her lack of unbiased distance and could only take her account of this people as un-reliable. She was astonished by their response because she found no difficulty in saying "we" as an adopted member of this culture while also saying "we" as an anthropologist. She had drawn closer to seeing with the eye of God.

The mysticism of knowledge rises from the desire not only to see all things as one but to see them in a deeper union with all other seers; to see all as one, to see as one.

The young anthropologist knew that the issue was not deciding which of the two knowledges she lived in was more reliable. Much less was she declaring that both knowledges are valid, as though she were advocating a kind of relativism. She understood that what all knowledges have in common is the yearning of its knowers for unity; it is this yearning that makes a knowledge possible and cannot therefore be expressed by way of it.

It is the not the mind that knows or the eye that sees, as we are reminded in the Upanishads, but the "mind of the mind and the eye of the eye." Although all our knowledge is the knowledge of the world of the *nafs*, the *nafs* itself actually knows nothing. The *nafs* is not the knower but the way the knower hides its deeper yearning from itself. The *nafs*, therefore, is what Nicholas calls the darkness that reveals that face which is beyond all veils.

THERE WERE TIMES when the Bonne Pecheur was under full sail in a good wind that you simply couldn't resist climbing into the crow's nest, twenty feet or so above the deck. A strong sea as well made for a dangerous but thrilling ride. If the old schooner got her way she would catapult you wheeling and gasping out through what Melville called the transparent air into the summer sea. Once you learned to get a firm grip on one of the stays and find a balanced stance within the small space of the crow's nest, however, you could stop resisting and yield to the wild back and forth of the boat's rocking so completely as to think they were your movements as much as those of the boat and the water. You could quickly forget where you were. Melville was right. You could even forget you were at all.

I first read *Moby Dick* in college. When I got to the chapter called "The Mast-Head," I had to look up the words *Descartian* and *pantheism*. When I saw their meaning, I laughed out loud with recognition. Until I read this famous passage, comparing it to my own experience on the Bonne Pecheur, I had never even noticed the loss of separateness from the surrounding elements, that "the only life in thee, now" was the rocking of the ship, the sea, and the inscrutable tides of God.

But I noticed something Melville didn't describe: when you look down from this elevation, you can see the shadow of the sails on the water but strangely you can't see your own shadow. What you see instead are spikes of sunlight, refracted by the broken surface of the water, all pointing at an invisible but unmoving point. That point is your opposite. Where your shadow should be is a restless starburst of light, sometimes coming up from the depths, sometimes reaching into them. Everything is in motion: water, boat, sails, wind, sky, you most of all, first diving forward then swinging to the side and back again. But the invisible point that is you in the water moves not at all. It does not even seem to pass through the water. Hard as you try, you can't quite locate it. Sometimes you are sure it's below at some terrible depth, sometimes it must be above you, above the heavens as well, sometimes it is both and at the same time within you.

You see nothing but change when all you want to see is the changeless. Spikes of blue-green fire emanate from your nonself upward and downward at the same time. You are the seer then the seen, then both and then neither. What you cannot see is the center from which all things are seen to be what they are.

I FOLLOWED the mass of screeching ghouls, stoned pirates, evil bunnies, and cross-dressed dancing girls as they made slow progress toward a lounge at the end of the corridor where a live band was playing something that sounded like a terrorist attack on the building. With just the kind of heedlessness Melville warned against I found myself tossed into an ill-lit sea of bodies that had already reached an advanced high energy state of samsaric abandon. With the first stomps and twists, I felt somewhat restrained by my costume, but as I continued to leap and spin the deathwrap gradually transformed itself from shroud back to toilet paper. Nearby dancers began unwinding strips of it in a kind of game in which miles of tissue rotting with our collective sweat seemed to wind us into a higher nakedness. If my exposed identity surprised or amused anyone, it didn't show; it didn't matter either. Each of us had been so perfectly swallowed into the pandemonium that masks just became masks, egos just egos. It was as though a sleep, a dream, was on us, making pantheists of us all.

That I was now wearing nothing but my undies no one else noticed. I noticed that.

How Far We Are from God

For thirty years I sought God. But when I looked carefully,
I saw that in reality God was the Seeker and I was the sought.

AN ANONYMOUS SUFI

E VER duck hunt?" Bob asked.
"Nope."
Bob and I were at the summit of East Rock Park in
New Haven, leaning back against my Nash Rambler, looking
out at the changing oak and maple trees, the city below, and
the sound beyond the city. It was so clear you could see Long
Island, a dark thread stretched along the horizon. Bob was
born and raised on Long Island. He was the first person I
met at divinity school. Because of that and because we loved
to tell each other our remarkably different growing-up stories, we had become fast friends.

Not only had Bob lived all his life in the northeast, an
area of the country inherently more interesting to me than
the middle west, he had spent all his summers on a lake in
Maine where he learned to fish in wild rivers and hunt deer
and moose. He could fly a seaplane. He sometimes wore a
wolfskin jacket, from a wolf he had shot in Labrador. In the

winter, for God's sake. Most amazing of all, his godfather was Admiral Byrd.

"The hunting season opens next week. I could bring guns and decoys from home."

I knew Bob didn't mean it this way but his invitation came as a challenge. I had never killed anything with a gun. In fact, I had shot a gun only once, some Boy Scout event at a shooting range. I saw in his invitation a need to prove something to myself. Bob's casual enthusiasm for hunting made it impossible for me to tell him how I had stood for hours on the shore of Lake Michigan with my battered Army-surplus binoculars watching the great waterfowl migrations. What's more, I wanted the approval of a new friend. Could I kill one of those birds to get it?

"I know a great place for hunting. In Branford. You can almost see it from here." He pointed up the coast to the east. "What do you say, Carse?"

"Sure."

A couple of weeks later, as we left our class in New Testament, Bob grabbed my arm. "I was home this weekend and brought back all the gear."

"What gear?"

"The decoys and shotguns. Remember? I even found someone who would lend us a boat."

I hadn't forgotten. But I also couldn't shake the memory of long lines of birds skimming the water or soaring high above the lake in great lazy Vs. I guess I was hoping that Bob would forget.

"How's tomorrow?"

"O.K."

The next morning we tied the boat to the top of the Rambler and headed out to the sound.

It was a chill day with a light wind off the water, the sky an even gray. "Just what we want," Bob said, explaining that the lack of brightness would make it easier to pick out your bird and get an aim on it, the waves just lively enough to make the decoys look real. We drove down a private road to the gravel edge of the sound and began untying the boat. On both sides were large houses facing the water over long treeless lawns. Many of the windows had been boarded against winter storms but now, in the absence of much weather at all, they were strangely still, making you think of what was missing: the hollow sound of tennis balls on the courts behind, the voices of friends on each other's porches, children running up from the tidal pools with their plastic buckets, suntanned girls arching out over the gunwales of their sailing dinghies.

Then I saw the boys. I believe there were three of them. I noticed first that they were not moving. I may not have noticed them at all if it weren't for that. They were sitting in a small circle around a fire, about three houses down the shore. Hard to tell, they might have been thirteen, no more than fourteen. Not grown up, anyway. One of them was smoking. All three were turned toward us. They were more than motionless, they were frozen in awkward positions as if our appearance had somehow interrupted what they had been doing. Later, Bob said he hadn't really looked at them.

We loaded the boat with the decoys, threw the bag containing bread, bologna, chips, and Cokes in the bow, and shoved off. I rowed so Bob could hold the guns on his lap and make sure the boxes of ammunition stayed out of the water that was collecting rapidly around our feet. We pulled up on a small flat rock of an island about two hundred yards offshore. It looked as though it had been designed for duck hunting. Bob had a neat trick of throwing the decoys out into the water so that their weighted strings swung free.

"Which gun do you want?" Bob asked, holding them both up.

"Bob, this is a hell of a time to admit it, but I've never shot a gun like that."

"What have you shot?"

"A twenty-two."

"Same idea," Bob said. He slowly went through the way you load each barrel and close the gun, making sure the safety's on. "Go ahead. Take a few shots."

I guess I had expected too violent a kick against my shoulder, so that when I pressed the trigger I pulled the barrel far out of aim. Bob patiently showed me the routine. He put his arm gently across my shoulders as he pointed out the features of the gun and the standard method for holding and shooting it: keep your left elbow pressed back, your right out level, and don't focus your eye on the sight, focus on the bird through the sight. Depending on the speed of the bird and its distance, you have to lead it, say, five to ten yards. I took a few more shots, drawing the imagined landing of the duck behind the sweep of the gun barrel.

"Now we wait."

We sat for five minutes, scarcely talking. Nothing was happening. I asked him if he liked the way our class in New Testament was going.

BOB WAS RAISED an Episcopalian, I a Presbyterian. From the way he talked about it, his God was decidedly more genial than mine. Mine was a distant, faceless entity you had somehow to find on your own. Bob's was always there ready to cheer you up. I thought of Bob's dad, an older, aristocratic gentleman with bushy, white eyebrows, abounding in genuine human warmth, ever glad to see you if only for the sake of a new joke—always a clean one. Bob didn't seem to have to look anywhere at all. His God was always checking in with you. So you just wait. And God's there.

My God was more like the sky over the sound: gray, vast, cold, full of veiled threat. You had to be a sharp thinker for this one and you had to work at it to get close. Getting close required dedication, sacrifice, and vigilance. For Bob's it was enough just to be there for morning worship, according to the Book of Common Prayer. Whether you come late, doze a little, even let your mind wander, it's all the same.

I wanted a God I could experience in some amazing way. Bob's faith overlapped so completely with his life that God was more like a companion than, well, like God. Such an experience of God seemed to me too unexceptional, too ordinary, reassuring but boring. I was always looking for a revelation, a sign, an appearance in the void so unexpected it threw off all your thinking. There was something lovely in the idea of a God who just puts an arm across your shoulders, but still, I wanted to be carried up, swept away.

There was an irony here I missed completely. If the God implicit in Bob's faith was an affable aristocrat, there was at least an openness to every sort of experience. No one in his variety of Christianity was privileged by the quality of their private relation to the Divine. My idea of the experience of God, on the other hand, led to religious elitism. In wanting a special revelation of my own, I wanted also to be special among the citizens of faith. The certainty I longed for would, I thought, give my voice a discernible authority—a direct route to spiritual arrogance.

I was impatient with Bob's lack of theological earnestness. My Presbyterian conviction that in time everything could be explained, even if current explanations were still incomplete, seemed to amuse him. I challenged him on it.

"You just can't attach your faith to any old theology," I argued. "You've got to have a theological context that will help you understand what your faith means and how to live by it. In fact, whether we realize it or not, Bob, our faith is already full of theological assumptions."

"That sounds like hermeneutics to me," Bob responded, pronouncing the word with exaggerated academic inflection.

"Well, there are some hermeneutical issues here, Bob, but basically I think we have to go beyond hermeneutics. It's really a question of knowing what's true and what isn't."

"Ducks! Look, right *there*. No, a bit more to the southeast. Don't show your gun." The gun. For a moment I had forgotten I was holding it.

They flew a high cautious circle over us then banked, swinging around to the north, dropping. Pintails and canvasbacks. Maybe a few grebes. Teals. A solitary merganser. Some twenty in all. As they came toward us, not fifteen feet above the water, I could see the indecision in their uneven wing beats. A secret alarm must have sounded, for they swept abruptly up and away from us, out of range in seconds.

ONCE, ON A FREAKISHLY hot day in early September, Bob and I were driving through the center of New Haven, gently arguing about the issue of Jesus' messianic self-consciousness. We had just come from New Testament class where we heard the professor say that scholarly consensus fell roughly on the negative side of the question: the likelihood was that Jesus never had a thought that he might be the messiah, much less the Son of God.

"It's a bunch of hermeneutics," Bob said. "But I guess I still agree with it." I was stunned that he could give away so much so easily.

I favored a midwestern, no-nonsense, Calvinist view that the Gospels mean what they say and that even if there are only a couple passages where Jesus seems to point directly to his messiahship, a couple passages are all you need. I was only in my first semester of Greek and we hadn't even come to the subjunctives, so I could hardly evoke much New Testament scholarship in support of this opinion, but, on the other hand, I couldn't quite accept the fact that Jesus didn't know exactly what he was saying and doing.

"The light's green," Bob said.

I quickly shifted into first and popped the car forward, stalling it. I started it and jumped out again but by now the light was already changing back so I hit the brakes and shifted into reverse. A line of pedestrians, annoyed as much by my indecision as by the heat, staggered into the intersection.

"The gospel's the gospel, Bob. There's a core to it that's always been clear to the Church and must have been clear to Jesus as well."

A man weighing three hundred pounds or more, his tightly buttoned suit dark with sweat, stared anxiously into the windshield of the Rambler, then stepped back onto the curb. He tugged a large white handkerchief out of a back pocket and patted his dangerously flushed face with it.

"What's the Greek word for it? *Kerygma*. Proclamation. The gospel is to be proclaimed first, Bob, studied later. That Jesus is the Son of God is essential to the kerygma. Always has been."

"Carse, see that big fella there, sweating through his polyester suit?"

"Yeah?"

"I'll wait for you in the car while you go proclaim your kerygma to the guy."

A brief scene played through my imagination: "Sir," I say, "I would like to declare to you the gospel of Jesus Christ." Since I am blocking his passage across the street, he stands before me, helpless, puzzled, miserable, his only evident desire to get me out of his life. I open my mouth to continue but nothing comes out, not a word.

"Green again, Carse. Get this bomb moving before we bake to death in it."

I gunned toward the next light. Bob turned to me and winked. "You missed your chance. Opportunities like that come rarely in life."

Bob's little joke had an uncomfortable edge to it. Barely into my first year of studying Christian thought, I had already come to believe that the world needed nothing more than to hear the gospel. But is that what this man needed? For all I knew he needed nothing more than to get out of the heat, kick off his shoes, and sit back with an iced tea. Maybe he also had an awful job, high blood pressure, and impossible financial burdens he was desperate to deal with. Or, it could be that he was perfectly content with what he did and who he was. With Bob's playful jibing I began to see that by assuming he needed the gospel before I had any knowledge of his life, I had lost my curiosity about him. My use of the gospel had not opened the world to me; it had narrowed my vision of it.

Spiritual arrogance is hardly unique to Christianity. I imagine I could just as easily have argued that this perspiring and unhappy citizen needed nothing so much as the Buddhist dharma, or the five pillars of Islam, or the ritual instructions of the Yajur Veda, or the wisdom of the Torah.

Mystics frequently warn us against seeing the whole world from a perspective unique to our own tradition. Ibn Arabi, a master of Sufi gnosticism, observed that if we remembered that "the water takes its color from the vessel containing it," we would not interfere with the beliefs of others "but would perceive God in every form of belief." But how do we get at the clear water? How especially can we presume to find God everywhere without arriving at an even higher arrogance?

There is a clue to answering this delicate question in the scholarly discussion of Jesus' messianic self-consciousness. As important as this question is for Christians, the fact is that there is no way of knowing for certain what Jesus thought of himself. The text is unclear. The best we can do is to develop an opinion but admit that support for it is ambiguous. Like all sacred texts, the Gospels have become a vast and patchy background against which we can do no more than project our experiential certainties and favored theories. What we see there is less the Gospels than the limitations of our own vision as it is profiled against their boundlessness. If we were to exercise Eckhart's "higher ignorance" here, we would pay less attention to what we know of the Gospels and more to the particular limitations that shape that knowledge.

Because it is the very opposite of spiritual arrogance, such ignorance has the effect of opening ourselves to the world. The clear water in Ibn Arabi's image is an unclouded knowledge of the world as it is. It is seeing God everywhere, or, as Nicholas of Cusa put it, it is seeing everything as God sees it. The clear water of that knowledge is contained in the particular vessel each of us receives from our tradition, but we remain unaware of it until we can begin to know the color our vessel has given it. Only by first seeing our own limitations can we learn to see the infinite variability of the world's colors.

Sitting in silence on that rock in Long Island Sound, waiting for ducks to show themselves against the gray and patchy sky, it would never have occurred to me that my view of the world was filtered through the peculiar colors of my midwestern background and the Christianity I had recently begun to study. The revelation I thought I wanted would only have validated that singular view. A revelation did come later that afternoon but it was not at all what I expected. I could not have anticipated the pain of it.

"GET DOWN," Bob whispered. "Here they come again. Safety off. Ready? Now! Fire!"

All I can remember of this moment is the electric reaction of the birds. In a second, they had doubled their speed and were gone.

"Carse, you got one!"

I scanned the surface of the water. There was a dark, inert object about fifty yards away.

"That's mine. Yours is over there."

Then I saw the bird. It was swimming vigorously, first this way, then that, awkwardly raising one of its wings. I recognized its unmistakable profile.

"What happened?"

"You hit it in the wing."

Suddenly the bird stopped moving. Motionless as the decoys, it seemed stunned. I had the wild hope that it was gathering its energy. Maybe it would do what mergansers do, start that long takeoff, beating its wings on the water, then rise into its remarkable arrowlike flight. It remained where it was, rocking listlessly on the waves. Something in me knotted and pulled back as I began to see what I had done. I put the gun down and closed its safety lock.

"What do we do now?"

"Now we wait. We'll have to see how injured it is. If it doesn't die by itself we'll go after it in the boat. This is when you need a dog."

The bird disappeared then came up again trying to lift its broken wing. It dived again. We waited.

"Merganser. It's a red-breasted merganser," I found myself saying out loud.

Bob turned sharply. "What? I thought you never hunted before."

"I haven't," I said, but couldn't bring myself to explain how I knew about mergansers.

Minutes passed without a sign of the bird.

"Where is it?"

"When they know they're dying they sometimes dive to the bottom and grab onto seaweed until they drown. You never get them when they do that."

We scanned the surface of the water. Finally, Bob shrugged his shoulders, jumped in the boat, and rowed out to retrieve his bird.

We sat on the island another hour or so, Bob's pintail laid out on the rock in front of us. He had shown me where the shot entered its neck and breast. "Not bad," he said. "Not so hard to clean when you kill it that way."

I was surprised to see how the sharp markings of the pintail in flight or on the water seemed to have faded. I'm not sure I could have identified it dead. I thought of the way pintails look in the water with their elegant upright necks and stately posture, their showy tail feathers spiking out behind. I thought again of the mergansers' flight, heads stretching forward as though they couldn't get there fast enough. Then I remembered the boy standing on a bluff high above the lake with his ill-focusing binoculars and I saw more clearly the violation I had just committed. I overrode a vision of beauty with a need to prove something about my manhood. Instead of quietly beholding what showed itself around me in all the colors of its mysterious otherness, I acted against its natural spontaneity, reducing it to a dull mass. This, too, was an expression of spiritual arrogance.

I stared out at the gray continuity of water and sky. They seemed to have nothing more to announce. The decoys continued to rock hypnotically. Now and then there was a drop of rain. We ate our sandwiches in silence. Bob pronounced the word *hermeneutics* one more time but said nothing about it.

Deciding it was time to collect the decoys, Bob stood and stretched.

"My God, look!"

I knew what it was even before I turned toward the shore, because I could see the red glow reflecting off Bob's rain jacket.

Two houses were on fire.

Like the silent tongue of God, the flame seemed to come from a million tiny sources then pull into itself and up, and still up, a hundred feet or more, a single joyous shaft laughing upward, eager to speak its one word. The houses, visible now only as darkened frames, were racing each other to join this exaltation, the fire now sucking breath through the black holes all the windows had become. The houses on either side were eyeing the fire with fire of their own, their walls lit with the first glow of this communion. Before we could take another breath, these houses had joined the gleeful, samsaric race, their flames chasing the others heavenward. Seconds gorging on decades.

Somewhere, miles back in the village, a siren started its coded alarm, spreading the news, calling out the volunteers who in less than fifteen minutes would stand in dumb respect as the final, lazy tongues rose and fell in the heaps of blackened timbers.

I started rowing in, pulling frantically at the oars, though I knew there was nothing we could do. Halfway I stopped and turned again. The two outer houses were now nearly invisible in the flames. Then I saw one of the boys. And another. They were running perilously close to the burning houses, their figures in dark profile against the fire. A third boy appeared from behind one of the houses. As though challenged by the others, he dashed up to the flames and back, ducking and sidestepping through the cascade of burning embers.

As I watched the boys, I realized I was watching something in myself. The willful destructiveness that lit the match also pulled the trigger. For a terrifying moment, I knew I could do one as easily as the other.

I turned back to Bob. Though he sat at the rear of the boat with an expression of wordless horror, I saw that for him all this had a different meaning. Bob was not out here killing birds; he was simply hunting. He seemed to find an inherent beauty in the whole of the activity—the guns, the decoys, the weather, the suspense, the camaraderie of the hunters. Shooting ducks had its own history for him; it was part of a larger family culture. He brought me out to the sound simply as an act of friendship. Whatever pain he experienced at that moment, it was not the pain of self-recognition.

Self-recognition is what the Sufi described who said that after a lifetime of seeking God he looked carefully and saw that he was not the seeker but the sought. In reality he was not a seeker at all; he was in flight from God. Only when he acknowledged this could he see that God was pursuing him. I had no perception that gray November afternoon that I was being sought, but I did have a changed awareness of myself as a seeker.

The revelation I had longed for was of God; the revelation I got was of a self I did not want to be. What I had hoped would be the experience of God's closeness was, because of the grief at what I had done and could not undo, the experience of being at a great distance from God. But seeing how far we are from God, the mystics thought, is the way God begins to seek us.

WE WERE the only witnesses but we had nothing to tell the volunteer firemen. I thought of the boys. Should I mention them? One was smoking and, of course, they were sitting around a fire. I was sure enough of that. And then there was the way they stared at us. That stare said a lot. But we did not really see them *do* anything. Besides, Bob didn't get a good look at them and they were too far away for me to identify them.

The real reason I made no mention of the boys was something very different. It was what I saw in the last one to appear from behind the flames. This one taunted the fire, racing one direction then another, leaping into the air, spinning, imitating the flames, all at breathless speed. It was a picture of unchecked joy. I recognized this figure but it would be many years before I had a name for it. It was my *nafs*.

Like a Random Bear

By God, I detest poetry. In my eyes there is nothing worse.

SUFI POET JALAL AL-DIN RUMI

T HE SPRING lies near the foot of the hill behind the house, under a stand of arching birches just like the trees in Robert Frost's famous poem. In the winter, bent by freezing rain, birches sometimes remain bowed after the morning sun has loosened the ice, which falls and forms heaps of crystal so dazzling "you'd think the inner dome of heaven had fallen." From the house we can see their white arches outlined through the hemlocks.

Near the end of the summer, I noticed that the water had begun to taste the way earthworms smell. It was time to check the spring, a task I had neglected for ten years or more. The spring empties into a well dug sometime around 1770. About ten feet deep, it is lined with fieldstones and loosely covered with aging timbers. It's easy to neglect checking it because you would rather not know what has fallen or crawled into it, or worse, taken up residence in it since the last time you got in there to clean out its clotted and decaying organic matter. Floyd and Tony, members of the volunteer fire department, came out from town with one of their pumps. When we got to the spring, we could see why the water tasted like earthworms. The planks had given way under what seemed to be a heavy weight and had largely disappeared into the dark stew the water had become.

"That's bear," Tony said, studying the damage. "No deer'd make it out of that."

Floyd began fishing woodsy debris out of the sump left by the bear's carelessness. It was filled mostly with several seasons of birch leaves, but there were a few featureless masses that, Floyd said, "you'd rather taste than take a close look at."

When we had pumped out enough muck and water to see the bottom, I volunteered to climb down into the well since I had on my sneakers and didn't mind standing knee deep in what was left. As I began cleaning slime off the walls with a broom, I noticed that the spring did not bubble up from the bottom as I had expected but oozed through the stones in a dozen or more places. All around me thin, vigorous rivulets of water were making clean streaks down the walls.

There was an especially lively source about eye level. I poked at the spot where it seemed strongest, enlarging the opening, then squinted into it, trying to see where the water came from. All I could see was more water. I don't know what I'd expected. Did I think the spring comes out of something the way water in the house comes out of the tap? I wondered if this was the spring itself, or was it just the water that comes from the spring? It was what we call the spring. But how far back would you have to go to find the actual spring, the absolute source of this ceaseless flow?

If we could track it back into the mountain, would we find that each of its paths led to more paths until all paths became invisible and we had nothing but the mountain itself and the sky above it?

"You got three, four gallons a minute down there," Tony said. "Easy."

"They say this spring hasn't dried up in two hundred years or more," Floyd added.

I looked up. They were staring down at me. Above them the canopy of birches was doing something magical with the sunlight. The inner dome of heaven.

IN HIS PUBLIC appearances Robert Frost used an odd expression: "Let me say this poem to you." He never "read" his poetry or "quoted" it. Since the tone and inflection of his voice scarcely changed when he began to "say" a poem, it took on a conversational quality. It did sound as though he were saying something to us and not merely reciting or repeating it.

Nonetheless, he always had the book open to the poem and was "saying" exactly what was written on the page. It certainly looked like he was reading it. In fact, on the several occasions I was in the audience, he never changed a single syllable or overlooked so much as a comma in these "sayings." He even gave the page number of the poems before he said them.

His audiences came to expect another idiosyncratic practice. I remember clearly the first time I witnessed it. An obviously adoring undergraduate student asked him what he meant by the famous lines:

And miles to go before I sleep,
And miles to go before I sleep.

She wanted specifically to know why he'd written the same line twice. Frost paused, as though trying to decide what to do with a question he must have been asked a hundred times, then looked down at the student with an ambiguous expression, opened his book to a certain page, and "said" the words:

And miles to go before I sleep,
And miles to go before I sleep.

Then, while threads of uncomfortable laughter trailed through the audience, he waited for the next question. The undergraduate stared blankly into her notebook.

This seemed as disingenuous as his "sayings." It was a way of making the point that what he wrote in the poem was sufficient, that if he had wanted to say something else, he would have said something else. Still, Frost knew that when he said these lines back to her they took on a very different meaning from whatever they had when he first wrote them. There was a meanness in his response. Besides being mean and disingenuous, it was contradictory. If Frost wanted the student to understand that the words of the poem meant just what they said, then why didn't he say just what he really meant? Why didn't he simply tell her it was a stupid question and he was tired of hearing it?

At the same time, I realized that my unasked question to Frost—why didn't he speak straight to us like he claimed?—

was the stupidest question of all. Frost was playing a trick on us and he knew it. Moreover, he knew that we knew it. And because we did, we were conspiring with him to keep the trickery going. Still, I wanted to know why he was playing this trick and what it was all about. Why did he persist in using this transparent maneuver with one audience after another? I believe that the discomfort in the audience's laughter at the student came from our suspicion that behind this obvious trickiness there was a deeper trick we didn't get. For all his insistence on "saying" the poetry in that famous nonpoetic voice, we sensed there was something here that remained unsaid. And what had to remain unsaid was the poetry itself.

That Frost never hid this palpable fakery in his personal appearances reinforced the suspicion that there was a deeper intentionality in it. He had, in fact, made quite a road show out of himself. Although he regularly offended members of his audience, he was careful to do it with a kind of stagy charm. He was Robert Frost appearing in the role of "Robert Frost, American Poet."

When John F. Kennedy asked Frost to say a poem at his inauguration in January 1961, any number of commentators were fooled into thinking this was the new president's way of honoring a great American poet and one of his personal heroes. Anyone familiar with Frost's public performances saw it differently. This was simply a master showman not missing the chance to expand his audience. If Kennedy thought he was honoring the old man, then he too was tricked. The boyish Kennedy and the avuncular Frost were both theatrical wizards, but Kennedy underestimated the size of the poet's persona. It was not Kennedy generously including Frost in his show but Frost slyly admitting the new president to his.

What was Frost up to? Why would a poet this canny be so conspicuous at playing "the poet"? Why would he repeatedly feign originality? Each time I heard Frost, the question recurred. The patent superficiality raised the same question as the spring: are these words the poetry or is the poetry in these words? If so, where does that poetry come from? To answer by saying the poetry comes from the poet is like saying the spring comes from the well.

It was what I would now call the mysticism of his poetry that carried me as an undergraduate from one of his performances to another. The immediate issue was the origin of the poetry itself. At another level, it was the issue of creativity, of knowing how to open to the deeper source within ourselves. Maybe the real trick here, I thought, was that Frost knew how to find this source and that somehow he was showing us how to find it as well.

I RAN MY FINGERS along the seams between the stones until I found the most vigorous flow of water. While its quantity was impressive, I was still a little disappointed. I think I wanted jets, hissing showers of stinging force, something showier than this. But I noticed when I jammed my finger into the outlet the flow immediately appeared somewhere else. This suggested a different kind of power. It was not a matter of pounds per square inch but of patient indifference to its path. Because it did not care where it went, it always had somewhere to go. We could have filled the well with earth and stone or capped it with concrete; we could have put an entire mountain on it and it would have continued to flow— somewhere. In fact, it had an entire mountain on it already.

This is the deepest secret to its living water: it transforms every obstruction into a new expression of itself. It accepts as channel what is presented as barrier. The mountain does not stand in the way of the spring; it is the way of the spring.

Little wonder that springs are sacred. We cannot live without the purity and regularity of springs. But it is not just this that makes them sacred. It is their indifference to us, that they come and go without the least interest in our well-being. We have no choice but to adapt ourselves to their unpredictability but they adapt themselves to nothing. They can vanish without a trace in one season and return to profligate vitality in the next. What we want from a spring is not just the minimal substance of life; we want possession of its final mystery: the source that is deeper and closer than both life and death.

AT FIRST, I framed my question about the origin of poetry like this: if Frost were really saying his poems, then everything he said outside his poems would be poetic. I tried to imagine him doing something ordinary like going to the supermarket. Would he jabber idly with the cashier? Or would he say something so rare and beautiful that she would freeze with rapture, unable to ring up his groceries?

Knowing nothing of Frost's private life, I kept a watchful eye on his performance. I was curious to see if, like a character in a play of Bertolt Brecht, he would step out of his role to tell us how he got the idea for a certain poem. He was walking an unfamiliar forest path, late for lunch, when he found himself at an unmarked fork. The thought was withering. I had a picture of Frost dashing off the line "One could do worse than be a swinger of birches," pushing his chair back, and saying to himself, "Now, damn it, there's a poem for you. Wait 'til they read this in Cambridge and New Haven."

My worry was that I would catch someone standing behind the poet, a soulless manipulator thrusting his public image at us with grim, unpoetic seriousness. It would be like finding a spigot emerging from the stone wall of the spring: no real originality here, just artifice.

Later I came to hear the rumors of Frost's offstage/off-page life. He was said to be an unreliable friend, a wrathful teacher, a disastrous father. Reports were that he could be cruel, obsessively pecunious, vain, self-absorbed, cold. This seemed to confirm the suspicion that at bottom Frost was all ego, a calculating self-promoter.

On reflection, I was surprised to find these rumors reassuring. Instead of the manipulative genius I had taken him to be, maybe he was more like a random bear never knowing when the solidity underfoot would give way to boundlessness and, more important, never caring. Can it be that the creative lies not in the acquired abilities of the ego but in the freedom to let the ego float off like so much woodsy refuse?

The most available metaphor I had for understanding this as an undergraduate came from the experience of drinking. I had been impressed less by the feeling of drunkenness itself than by the fact that there was some part of me the alcohol never touched. The self that knew I was drunk was not itself drunk. I remained a silent watcher of myself, soberly aware of my own silly and often dangerous behavior. This adolescent discovery takes a larger meaning in adult experience: at the heart of all our passions—grief, joy, alarm, lust—resides a clear-eyed witness ever awake and innocent, untouched by these storms.

Could it be, I wondered, that behind Robert Frost's enigmatic public presence there was an undisturbed center, an imperturbable passivity, that kept a heron's eye on what he did and what was done around him without being captured by it? If so, this could explain why such beauty could come through an ego as pinched and combative as Frost's.

It is clear to me now that my curiosity about Frost was caused by more than the irreconcilability of his poetry with his personality. The more compelling question, and one that remains a question, is how I or anyone can open the sources of creativity within ourselves, given the obvious limitations of our worldly entanglements. The easier, more manageable answer to this question would be that creativity is a skill or a technique, a certain activity we could be taught if we were bright and clever enough. In my brief exposure to Frost I sensed a radically opposed alternative: creativity is *not* doing something, it is looking through whatever we do with the eye of the sleepless watcher, it is remaining through whatever we say an uncritically receptive listener. W. H. Auden said that we become poets not because we have important things we want to say but because we "like hanging around words listening to what they have to say." True creativity stands aside so each word, each form, can emerge with its own energy. True creativity leaves the question of its origin unresolved.

When I began to see it this way, Frost's response to the student took on a very different meaning. The cruelty of his treatment of her was thrilling because we could see by the ease and speed with which he expressed it that this old man was reeling, out of control, unable to rescue his personality from its inherent heedlessness. It was a drunk's vicious reaction to a minor provocation. At the same time, the sober watcher must also have been in this exchange. If so, Frost needed the undergraduate. She was his perfect audience. He needed her question to stay in serious contradiction with himself. For a stunning moment, the two of them seemed to have entered into an intimacy that excluded the rest of us. When she looked down at her notebook, could it be, therefore, that she was ashamed not of her inadequacy but his? Was Frost telling her, in the only way he could say it, that he had the same question? If there was a trickiness in his being a poet, then the trick was on him as well.

WE CAN'T LIVE without springs. Neither can we live without wells. We can't stand on a damp spot in the woods and expect to absorb the water through the soles of our naked feet. The well must be built before the waters of the spring are of use to us. Of course, building the well makes no change in the spring itself. The change is all on our side. Well building is a complicated strategy of adjusting our life to the life of the spring. My long-forgotten predecessors on this land knew that only with a large range of skills, hard labor, wide-awake vigilance, and good luck could they ever hope to share in these living waters. The choice was obvious: build it right or die.

On the hill above the well the remains of a foundation are barely visible. From the dimensions of the site we can surmise that a part of the present house was first built there and later moved down the hill to its current location. Why it was moved no one knows, although it is a reasonable guess that an earlier well had been dug into the hill above the old foundation. When this well failed or was found inadequate, it made a new well necessary. Because the house had to be downhill from the well, it was also necessary to move the house.

The forgotten builders, living close to the edge because of the poor soil and the brutal winters of the New England mountains, knew they could survive only if they matched the impermanence of the natural elements with an impermanence in their own strategies. They knew how to build for the centuries but they were ready to unbuild for the seasons. The well builders in whose work the springs stayed freshest were those whose work was both most permanent and most dispensable. Building and unbuilding were not opposed activities; they were the same activity.

FROST WAS a master builder of word walls. He had learned the assorted techniques of putting words together in a way that made them look like poetry. But learning the techniques of poetry does not by itself make great poetry any more than building a well guarantees the vitality of the spring. Just as the poet has to let the ego step aside, technique too must be abandoned at just the right moment, allowing the poetic to enter on its own terms. The question then is whether we can find in the masterful construction of Frost's poems the point where their unbuilding begins. Does his work carry a testimony to its own impermanence? Can we see this in "Stopping by a Woods"?

One of the first clues is the transparency of the writing, as in nearly all of Frost's poetry. To be sure, the technique is always right in front of us. His work is written in verse, it often rhymes, it is precisely metered, so it looks like poetry. Still, the technique does not draw attention to itself as technique. His verses don't say, This is a poet speaking. This is largely because of the naturalness of his speech, his ability to hang around words to hear what they have to say. As a result, his words so often point away from themselves at lucidly seen realities: a child's grave, the path not taken, a crow on a snowy branch. They mirror these realities with such clarity that we don't notice the mirror itself. By now the technique has hidden itself.

None of his poems is more transparent than "Stopping by a Woods," and none is more studied, catalogued, or memorized. Yet, for all its simplicity, for all the availability of its images, it is with what we cannot see, what we do not hear, that the poem is concerned.

The poem begins with the falling snow. Its initial descriptions are of unambiguous objects, plainly viewed: a wood, the horse, a meadow. Light and dark sharply profile each other. In fact, the poem itself falls like snow. Its simple words drop without color and weight. There is no noise in this writing.

As the snow continues the edges blur, the darkness grows, the visual spaces fill. The result is that we are ourselves emptied of visual content. There is nothing to see. In the very middle of the poem falls a line that abruptly ends the outer vision: "The darkest evening of the year."

This simple phrase, ordinary as fieldstone, cannot be removed without the whole work collapsing. Yet it begins the unbuilding of the previous lines. The poet has stopped to look at snow falling in a woods but if it is this dark there is nothing to see. The phrase is placed directly against the apparent flow of meaning. Does meaning emerge somewhere else?

Turned away from the wood, the poet turns inward. So do we. But as we do, we find there is something irresistible there as well, requiring us to move on, keeping us from sleep. Just as there is nothing to hold our attention from without, there is nothing to hold it from within and we turn away from that as well. But toward what?

The poem hints at neither destination nor direction. We know only that there are many miles—an indefinite distance opening before us into the immeasurable dark. Although we must go, there is no point to our going. By the end of the poem we have become the watcher who cannot sleep and the traveler who cannot arrive.

The poem has the character of a Zen koan: a word or phrase that speaks but says nothing. An effective koan is unforgettable, and yet uninterpretable—or, the same thing, endlessly interpretable. Its spiritual function is to show us that the mind is empty, that its content is attached to nothing beyond itself. Thoughts come and go, weightless as snowflakes, shapeless as wind.

Although this poem is among the most unforgettable poems in the English language, its meaning always eludes us. Mountains of interpretation have accumulated around it but have done nothing to capture it. It continues to ooze through all our attempts to contain it and to remain goalless, nameless, indifferent to our need for it.

Then where is the poetry in these lines? Certainly not in the intention of the poet, for he has backed away from telling us what he is saying—by saying no more than the words. Certainly not in the words, for they point away from themselves. Certainly not in the realities at which the words point, for those realities vanish into the outer dark. It must therefore lie between us and the poet, between us and the words. For that reason, the poetry that keeps us speaking and listening to the words is a poetry the words will never perfectly contain. The poetry is timeless, inexhaustible, the poem is not. Its words are like the stones in my well; the skill with which they have been placed cannot guarantee the spring will not someday go elsewhere. It may happen, for some it has already happened, that this poem no longer opens to the boundless. But the boundless remains, it will always remain, calling forth new builders and unbuilders.

WAS I RIGHT about Frost's ability to set his troubled personality aside for the sake of poetry? I was given the perfect chance to test the theory.

As Frost was being introduced at Kennedy's inauguration, he was led out of the shadows of the temporary seating into the brilliant sunlight of the speakers' platform. He stared briefly at the text of the poem before him then tried to shade it with his hand. It was quickly apparent that the angle of light on the manuscript made it impossible for him to see. It had been announced that he was to "say" his poem "The Gift Outright." But he would first "say" a long verse preamble composed for the occasion. This trick of the light forced him into the open. It was obvious at last that he could say his poems only because he had long since memorized them.

I could not have asked for a more perfect moment. I moved closer to the TV and studied Frost's face. How would he handle this awkward moment? The arc of his fame had reached its highest point, almost the highest point possible for a poet, and his show had failed him. Would he let his famed persona drift away with as little care as a boy might let a sapling leap toward the dome of heaven? Would we finally see the face of a true poet, as indifferent to its destiny as the face of the Buddha?

Rubbing the dust from the screen of our old black-and-white TV, I stared into the grainy electronic image of Frost's face, but the snowy haze of its poor reception blurred all edges and there was no way I could tell. Frost himself had become a koan, an unforgettable presence, one whose meaning will forever elude us—exactly like the Buddha.

"SURE YOU can swim all right in those sneakers?"

Looking up at Floyd and Tony profiled against the birches, I realized that the water was now nearly to my waist.

A Shared Silence

I've heard it said there's a window that opens from one mind
to another, but if there's no wall, there's no need for fitting a
window, or the latch.

JALAL AL-DIN RUMI

THE INVITATION to give a public lecture at my old
college had arrived a year in advance. Because it had
been extended so early, I knew they were expecting
a winner. They even sent me the honorarium a month before
the date. It was enough to buy the first new overcoat I'd had
since graduating ten years earlier. I took on the assignment as
if it were a second doctoral dissertation. I researched, composed, refined, polished, and refined it again, then rehearsed
it until the manuscript tucked in my briefcase was the best I
could possibly do.

I took my place behind the lectern and looked out at the
several hundred faces, mostly undergraduates, gathered in
the back of the auditorium. I squared the manuscript and
centered it on the angled surface, wondering whether to pull
the little chain on the antique lamp arching over the front
edge of the lectern.

A few former professors had taken seats in the crowd of students. I thought they looked abstractly pleased that one of theirs had become one of them. And there was Katz. He was sitting on the outside aisle, his legs crossed and pointed at the wall.

. As latecomers completed the ritual of finding someone to sit with, I gave the chain on the reading lamp a gentle tug. It didn't seem to work. A second more decisive jerk caused the entire device to flip back and swing away from the lectern. As I wondered whether to take another chance with it, something happened I most definitely had not expected. Making her way toward an empty seat in a mass of undergraduates was my mother.

Typically overdressed in a large black hat and white gloves, as though this were an elegant social occasion, she gleamed sweetly up at me like the whole event was just for the two of us. She must have decided that morning to leave her fifth-grade class with a substitute and make the two-hour drive down. As she later put it, she had never before seen me "perform in public."

I WON A FEW audible laughs, allowed scarcely a dozen sleepers, looked up frequently from the manuscript without getting lost, and finished on time to respectful applause. One professor briefly clasped his hands over his shoulder in a kind of victory gesture. But Katz had made his exit unseen.

I jumped into my car and followed my mother to a small local diner, anticipating the characteristically voluble expressions of her pride in me, certain I had earned them. Standing in the diner's parking lot, she gave my new coat an approving once-over, softly touched her cheek to mine, careful not to smudge me with her fresh lipstick, and walked into the restaurant on my arm. After complimenting the waitress on her hair, she ordered the businessman's special for both of us.

She asked about my children, told a long story about her two big smelly dogs, shared the latest adventures with her fifth graders, and brought me up to date on my brother and sister and their families.

An hour later she was in her car, explaining that when she stays away too long the dogs get mad at her and doodoo on the kitchen floor. She raised a gloved hand over the top of the car and flashed me a see-you-later as she wheeled smartly into the moving traffic. Not a word about the lecture, nothing whatsoever that resembled maternal pride in my "performance."

Not until I was headed home on the plane, hours later, did I discover that I had left my new coat hanging in the diner.

And not until my mother was long dead, years later, did I discover the mysticism in what she did not and could not have said. Within this pointless chatter over a businessman's special was hidden a gift of silence so originating not even the noise of death can be heard in it. I can see why I missed it. It was a lot easier for me to muse over the silence as I found it in Charlie or in the words of the poet. But the enveloping silence I entered into with my mother reached farther than to the source of speech and creativity.

"BE SILENT," Rumi said, "and practice the art of silence."
Silence is a way of being and it is something we do. Learning
to be silent is the goal of the art of silence. But since it is the
unspeakable that makes speech possible, we are already silent.
Silence is the essential condition of the soul. Becoming silent
is not, therefore, something we achieve but a return to what
we already are. Rumi could just as well have said, Be who you
are and practice the art of being who you are.

It has been said of Eckhart that he avowed to live "a life
in which the divine silence is never lost." Is the essential silence of the soul a divine silence? Is there a human silence?

The initial awareness of our silence is deceptively simple.
It begins with the obvious fact that when we are talking we
are not silent. But as we quickly discover when we stop talking, this truism deceives. We don't actually stop talking. It's
just that we are not talking out loud. Inwardly, the babble
doesn't cease. In fact, it seems even to increase as we pay
attention to it. Like a naughty child, we respond to every attempt to quiet ourselves by saying the very things our internal censor has tried to forbid. Characteristically, the first
attempts at internal silence only magnify the noise.

So the obvious fact that when we are talking we are not
silent yields to the more complicated fact that when we are
not talking we are still not silent. How then do we go about
the task of shutting down the inner voices that are trying to
get our attention?

It is possible to get ourselves to stop talking by talking to
ourselves, but only with virtuosic effort. We would need to
develop an inner discipline by which we are always ready to

spring out with a mental "Stop!" each time a word enters the edge of consciousness. This, however, would be less the practice of silence than the practice of shouting ourselves down. The result is something closer to mental wordlessness than to genuine silence. It is still the art of silencing, not the art of silence.

We won't make any progress in reaching a deeper level of silence until we abandon the struggle to silence ourselves and begin to listen to the many voices that insist on speaking within us. To do this we must become a listener who has nothing to say. Before we can become such a listener we must first know whose voices they are. In one sense, of course, they are all our own. There are no other speakers actually residing in us. In another sense, however, none of these voices is ours. They originate in our parents and children, in friends, lovers, teachers, in our critics and models, heroes and heroines. "Stand chin-to-chin with each of life's challenges and slug it out," my father says in one of his characteristic lectures. Dead thirty years, he is standing right at my shoulder. "It's better to lose than not to fight at all," he adds and gives me a gentle shove. "Will you miss me?" Alice asked a few days before she died, and continues to ask over and over again. Though the speakers are absent there is an urging, an insistent energy in their voices. These words don't just whip through our interiority like leaves in a storm. They require a response. "You know, I'm not really a slugger," I try to tell my father. "Yes, Alice," I say each time she asks. "Yes."

There is a paradox here. These words are spoken by others. We could not possibly have invented the words or the speakers. And yet, because no one is actually speaking them in us, they are also our own. When we step back to be a listener who has nothing to say, we see ourselves not just noisy with words but deep in conversation with scores of others. That we can have this conversation completely within ourselves shows how far we can isolate our interiority from others. None of the conversants need ever know we are talking with them. On the other hand, because every voice within us is someone's voice, we know this isolation can never be complete.

All language is therefore shared language. Even the most intimate and hidden conversation with ourselves is in words we have learned from speaking with others. In fact, we don't know what we are saying to ourselves unless we know what these words would mean if we spoke them to another. It is a curious fact that we cannot make up a private language to use only within ourselves. We might devise a secret code with an array of sounds and signs indecipherable to others, but if we couldn't translate them into language someone else could understand we couldn't make sense of them either.

For this reason, unless we have listeners other than ourselves, we cannot speak at all. I can't say anything to you unless you are waiting to receive my words. But I won't know I have said anything until you respond with your own speech. Then, of course, you won't speak unless my words have behind them a waiting silence of my own. Silence precedes our discourse with each other and makes it possible, but it must be a shared silence. Before each of us can have a voice of our own, we must enter a silence we can enter only together. It is a silence without walls.

By stepping back to be the listener who has nothing to say we discover that just as there is no language that is exclusively our own, there is no silence that is not a shared silence.

Because our speaking with each other implies a shared silence, because it is a silence that language cannot exhaust, the mysticism of language does not reside in what we say but in the very existence of language itself. Every spoken word is a threshold into our own inwardness and at the same time into oneness with others.

The soul has nothing to say. Its essential silence makes voices possible but it has no voice of its own. Therefore, from the perspective of soul, it is the ongoing, renewable, changeable nature of language, its continuing life, that is most important. Because the meanings of words arise in the way speakers respond to each other, there is a constant evolution of the meaning of any given word over the course of its use. The meaningfulness of our speech has much more to do with our ability to keep our discourse with each other open than it has to do with pinning down the meanings of words and expressions. We know our discourse is meaningful not by what we have said but by what has yet to be said. Soul draws our speech forward in the direction of the unspeakable. Only thus can it remain speech.

Ego, always the earnest dualist in us, is eager to maintain boundaries between speaker and listener. It wants to direct the flow of words, knowing in advance where our conversation with others is headed. A builder of walls, the ego longs for control over the meaning of words. But doing so, it walls itself in and though it may increase the volume of words it says less and less.

NO SOONER did the lecture invitation arrive than I started jotting down thoughts. At first they came in a chaotic tumble. When a reasonably coherent body of ideas began to accumulate, I knew it was time to bring up the faces of those I expected to be listening to this opus. I put Katz in the front row where he waited restlessly for ideas that would blow his hair back.

I gave the lecture an initial run-through before this phantom crowd. They proved to be a hard audience. Many of the ideas bored them, they had trouble with my professorial tone, I could be more convincing. There were many versions.

The manuscript I flattened out on the lectern that morning was the last of dozens I had rewritten under the critical eye of my imagined roomful of faces. Except for Katz positioning himself alarmingly close to the exit, I was heartened to see how nearly they resembled the interior audience with which I was already familiar.

The paradox of language was hard at work here. These voices were my own, for no one else was speaking in me. At the same time, these voices were not my own; I could not have invented one of them—even though, except for Katz and a handful of other former professors, they were people I had never met and would never meet. Katz's voice was, of course, the most familiar of all those from the past. His impatience with flaccid thinking had been too painful ever to forget. Still, not a single one of the comments his imagined presence was aiming at this lecture had I ever heard from him. The Katz who joined that anonymous audience was not retreating from some place ten years behind me. This was a Katz waiting just ahead, spelling out a set of expectations so precise that I had to throw away a dozen ideas for every one I thought might fit.

The oddness is that these voices did not originate in me; neither did they originate in my past. Instead their origin lay ahead of me: a huge auditorium of dynamic silences. I experienced these silences as expectations but they were not expectations that had already been expressed; it was what I expected them to expect. Where we touched was nowhere in time or space. It was not here or there, now or then.

Because of this silence I was able to say something I could never have found in the jabbering of my present inner discourse. Although the resulting thoughts were entirely my own, I could not have made them up by myself.

Looking back now, after nearly three decades of teaching, much sobered by the difficulty of teaching well, I can see how the mysticism of the occasion eluded me. If the invitation opened an inner circle and drew me into new reflection, I responded by trying to close the circle again. It was the ego that had taken over the writing of the lecture. The ego, as always, misunderstood the nature of this gift of silence. Its desire was to fill the silence with words so clear and authoritative they would leave the audience speechless. I wanted to bring them to their feet in applause, of course, but an applause that recognized the speaker's achievement in saying all that needed saying. I wanted to do to Katz what Katz did to me as a student. I thought I could do it if I spoke like Katz. What I didn't understand is that I could do this only if I listened like Katz. Katz built his own walls of words and often seemed to get lost behind them but he also depended on us to tear them down with our confused questions and comments, bringing our messiness into the tidy order of his thought, opening him to paths surprising to both him and us, opening us to new questions, deeper confusion, and awe at the limitless creativity of mind.

WHEN I FINISHED the lecture, I waited for a minute or so as the students gathered their coats and books and headed toward the exits, now thrown open onto the campus beyond. I walked down to greet some of the professors. There were warm handshakes and a few polite questions before they started back to their classes and office hours.

I read in their reactions that the morning had been a success. Although not much was said after the lecture, it was enough to assure me that I had correctly anticipated the expectations drawing me ahead all these months. I was confident I had shaped my ideas cleverly enough that they fit snuggly into the waiting silences. I was puzzled by only one thing: why I was so disappointed by my mother's response.

Her response was not a response at all. She seemed not to have heard one word of that lecture. I tried to explain to myself that she was not really at home in academic discourse and besides, these were not the kinds of ideas that would interest her. Still, I was shocked that the waitress's hairdo was more interesting to her than my whole "performance." Didn't she notice that I had a life of the mind? She didn't have to share in it, just peek through the little window I opened that morning and notice it was there. She was concerned less with the importance of this occasion to me than with her dogs' doodoo.

What I overlooked altogether that morning was the significance of her being there at all. She, too, had expectations but they were very different from those the college had. I could not have filled her expectations with that lecture or with any other. There was no amount of speaking that could satisfy the silence she brought with her because it was the silence in which I first received the gift of language.

I dreaded this silence. I was exposed by it. I wanted her to erase it with a few simple words of praise. A mere gesture of approval would have allowed me to fly back to New York that afternoon untroubled by the still unacknowledged fact that there was no soul in that lecture, only a skillful work of ego. In fact, she had listened to me. She was responding to what was much more real in me and not to the stylized academic I had placed behind the lectern. It was not her lack of response that troubled me. It was the difficulty of hiding myself from the deeper silence I recognized in that response.

There was something still more difficult. She came to me out of a silence but she also came into one. I learned to be a child in her presence, but she learned to be a mother in mine. I expected her to listen to me, to see who I truly was, but she expected to find the silence in which she had come to be who she was. And, of course, she did find it. It's always there. I knew it, too, because I was embarrassed by her silly hat and white gloves. She came to be beautiful before all those students and professors but the beauty was for me and she knew I knew that. We were beautiful for each other but it was a beauty neither of us could have by ourselves.

If I wanted to hide from the silence she brought with her, I wanted even more to hide from the silence she came to find in me. Most of all I wanted to hide from the fact that there is but one silence.

I thought at the time I was disappointed in my mother but, in truth, I was disappointed in myself. The lecture was so perfectly adequate it left almost nothing to be said. And for that reason, it said nothing. My mother did not hear me and neither did they. I had been drawn forward by a dynamic silence but the silence came to an end in my own speaking. I brought the right words but there was something missing in the speaker I came to be: a listener. All I had managed to prepare for all those anonymous faces was an anonymous face. The mask was just right but no one was looking at them through it.

My mother came to me with the silence in which I learned to be who I am. She also came to a silence in me I did not bring to the lecture. She taught me that by speaking well I practiced only the art of silencing others.

Losing the Way Is the Way

A lover came to the dwelling of the Beloved and asked to be admitted.

"Who is there?" the Beloved asked.

"I am here," the lover answered.

The Beloved refused to admit the lover. After wandering in grief and longing for years, the lover returned to the Beloved and begged to be admitted.

"Who is there?"

"You alone are there," the lover responded.

The door opened.

A SUFI STORY

CCORDING TO my mother, the way I was born," Gerry said, "is that she went to the A&P and when she came home I jumped out from behind the kitchen door and surprised her. I actually believed this until I took health ed in junior high."

Gerry, a college girlfriend, told me this while we were taking a break from studying in the library. It was a warm fall evening in the 1950s and we were seniors in a midwestern college. We were on our way to the A&W root beer stand in my Nash Rambler. I was telling her something about Don Hutson, all-time great end for the Green Bay Packers, when she

broke in with this peculiar little story. Why she told me at just
that moment I cannot imagine. It certainly had no connection
to Don, or with anything else we had been talking about.

Gerry laughed when she told me, not because of the oddness of the story but because she expected it to amuse me.
But it didn't amuse me. It had no impact at all. On the contrary, I found it so inane that I dismissed it at once, without
comment. So why then have I not forgotten it? Why do I
even recall such minute details as the way she interrupted my
story about Don Hutson, or that she told it just as I was turning into the root beer stand? Although I visited the place
dozens of times in my college years, I have no other specific
memory of being there. I even recall the exact intonation of
her voice and the way she was sitting in the far corner of the
front seat, wearing my Milwaukee Braves cap.

GERRY SAID her mother told her the story. I don't know if
this is true but it doesn't matter because, even if Gerry made
it up, it reveals how receptive the child was to stories of herself, especially of her origin. The child was beginning to see
the enormous difference between who she was becoming for
those around her and who she was in herself. She needed a
story to account for this discrepancy. We cannot have an
identity of our own until we have our own story. But it is also
by way of story that we know we need an identity. When
Gerry first heard this story she was just coming into that
need. She was in a state of narrative hunger.

In the tale Gerry told me, the child's story died in health
ed, by which I assume she meant she got "the facts." Then

why did she bother to tell it to me, even interrupting what she knew was for me a most important story about one of my very few heroes? She didn't indicate which facts were at issue here, didn't even seem to care. The story clearly had a life for her that the facts didn't.

I am not even sure why I tell the story here. You might say I was looking around for a story to illustrate something I wanted to say about mysticism. But, in fact, it didn't happen that way. The story appeared quite on its own without announcing itself as a mystical story. It popped up with as little connection to anything around it as when I first heard it. It has done this before, often. So it is not quite correct that I suddenly remembered the story. It is rather that I never really forgot it. The story has a life of its own. It elbows its way into whatever I am thinking whenever it wishes. I don't search for it; it comes after me. In ordinary speech I would say, "the story occurred to me."

The story came after Gerry as well. Even if it started with her mother, it had a persistent energy her mother could not have given it. It awoke a listener in Gerry's childhood that would not go back to sleep in her adulthood. But it awoke a listener in me as well. Why would a tale so contrary to fact and seemingly silly persist in seizing our attention unless there were a listener in us awake to something we could not yet notice?

STORY AND FACT are always in uneasy tension with each other. No matter how carefully we line up the historical data or how honestly we report the actual events through which we have lived, these do not by themselves tell the story of our lives. To tell all is not to tell a tale. Getting the facts straight is not enough to find the story to which they belong. In fact, getting the facts straight is a very different activity from that of finding a story that can be "faithful" to the facts.

The faithfulness of stories to fact is often the way we evaluate them. "Is that story true?" "Did that really happen?" But stories seem to have a life of their own that allows them to race on without so much as a glance at the factual.

Because of their inherent liveliness, stories command a sharper attention than facts, however appropriate facts may be to the matter under discussion. The way an audience is visibly awakened by a narrative example during an otherwise precisely factual lecture shows that stories touch us closer to a listener's center than accurate descriptions of objective states of affairs. Gerry would not have grabbed my Milwaukee Braves cap and slid over to her corner of the front seat to lecture on the mechanics of her conception and delivery, nor if she had would I have remembered. The mythic story of her birth was abruptly invalidated by a few physiological details but it obviously had far too much vitality to be buried by the truth.

A hint as to the deeper meaning of the myth of Gerry's birth is that birth and story have something in common: they both point to a mystery of origin. Answers to questions about where stories come from are as notoriously inadequate as the answers to questions about where babies come from. Good stories also jump out and surprise us.

TO ASK WHERE stories or babies come from is like asking where springs come from. Just as the spring always has a deeper source within itself, stories come from nothing else but other stories. A story becomes especially powerful when it displays the mystery of its own origin At the deepest level of any memorable story is the haunting presence of another story or maybe even many other stories. They echo in each other.

The myth of Gerry's birth shows its brilliance only when we listen carefully to its narrative resonance, only when we hear the deeper myths that sound and re-sound in it. In spite of its extreme brevity, this is a tale of essentially unlimited resonance.

It is a story of childhood prowess. A newborn leaps out from behind a door, a bold and calculated gesture full of advanced skill and a grown-up sense of theater. The myths of heroes' births are full of such amazing acts, like Hercules strangling deadly serpents in his cradle, or the Buddha dropping without warning from his mother's womb, radiantly dressed in princely armor, announcing his greatness to the universe.

The element of surprise in the tale itself holds mythic echoes. Surprise can lead to either delight or menace. Sarah caused laughter by giving birth to Isaac when she was at an advanced age. Jesus' birth occasioned both joy and terror. The unexpected appearance of the child Krishna was an erotic delight to the milkmaids but brought only jealous grief to their husbands.

If we see the newborn as a helpless babe in arms, dependent on those around her, we overlook one of the central features of birth narratives: this small being is a terror. Even her possible appearance threatens the existing order, causing the powerful to protect themselves by such desperate measures as locking wives and daughters away to prevent them conceiving an heir and competitor. Any number of tiny rivals have been abandoned to rivers and seas, sealed into cells and caves, left for dead in wastelands, set adrift on rivers. The pharaoh, King Herod, even the legendarily gentle Arthur of Camelot went so far as to slaughter an entire generation of children to make certain no babe would undo them. On first hearing Gerry's story, one might think the mother's reaction would be one of happiness. Maternal happiness, however, has no mythic depth whatsoever. From the mythic record, we know mothers are at high risk. Their offspring can sneak up on them with evil design, as in the case of the Babylonian urgoddess Tiamat. The hero god Marduk tricked Tiamat into opening her great maw, which he entered unseen. Then, in a fury, he destroyed her bone by splintered bone.

The mother at least appears in this story, however, and plays a crucial role, while the father is not even mentioned. This is a fatherless birth, an event that occurs only in the presence of women with no male assistance whatsoever. It is typical of the great birth myths that the father's role is either ignored altogether or forced to be played out of view like the Holy Spirit secretly entering the virgin's womb or Zeus sneaking through the bars of Danae's cell outlandishly disguised as a shower of gold. The father in Gerry's myth has been done away with as decisively as Oedipus' father Laertes, leaving only her mother to love, hate, or fear. If there is a miracle here, it is that the event defies all rational account. The fatherlessness of the tale is the primary mark of its triumph over rationality. It is another way of saying that my origin is not outside me and obvious, but within me and hidden.

The mother, on the other hand, although in some danger and with a doubtful connection to the daughter, is far more formidable than the father. Her enormity is clearly represented in Gerry's myth. She has come back from a journey to the A&P like Demeter with the seasonal fruits to greet Persephone at her emergence from the obscurity of Tartarus. Even grander, for she has come from the A&P, the Atlantic and the Pacific Tea Company, representative of the vast oceans that embrace us all, the beginning and the end, watery birth and watery death, like the serpent Ouroboros eternally consuming and giving birth to itself. The A&P is a supermarket, a higher exchange, an inexhaustible reservoir, a place so complete it can embrace its own contradictions: it is both abbatoir and garden, sacrifice and harvest, death and life. In the mythic record providing and consuming food often overlap. What the mother gives she can take away. The child is fed by the mother, literally eats the mother, but can also be eaten by the mother. Gerry surprises an unprepared mother but she is even less prepared for the surprises her mother might have for her.

She finds Gerry, after all, in the kitchen. Children know the kitchen as the place where you can be burned and cut but also fed and mended. Myth knows the kitchen as a hags' workshop where knife and fire are the chief media, where small animals and children are chopped up and brewed into magical concoctions and potions.

And where did Gerry hide? Behind the door, the portal, the gates, the locus of ceremony: "Lift your head, O ye gates, that the King of Glory may come in!" The door is also a symbol of passage, a boundary between realms, a line of no return, a threshold of irreversible loss: "Abandon hope all ye who enter." It is a barrier at which one age meets another, and the pathway through which one age becomes another. It is a site of hostility but also of hospitality. Just as it can lock away the old it can open to the new: "Knock and it shall be opened." What it opens to we can never know before we knock.

From the fact that the resonance in Gerry's birth story is essentially bottomless we learn not that it was so remarkable a tale but that even the most usual stories around which our lives shape themselves are rich with echoes of deeper tales. Our self-understanding has a thoroughly narrative character. The self we know is a self on the way, a self in the midst of its passage.

Mystics speak frequently of the mystical path, the narrative journey of the soul to the One. It never happens that the lover goes directly to the dwelling of the Beloved and is admitted at once. Because the lover is mistaken about the goal, a long and transforming journey is required before a return to the Beloved is possible. This journey, as Eckhart says, is nothing other than "life itself." To understand the narrative character of one's own life is therefore to understand its inherent mysticism.

DECADES PASSED and I decided I would go back to that college for a scheduled class reunion. Except for the public lecture I had delivered there a few years after I started teaching, this was to be my first visit.

It was a hot, clear day with just a hint of an afternoon thunderstorm. Small groups of alumni drifted onto the large lawn, looking. I approached a gathering of people under a sign for my graduating year. A young man seized my hand like I was a lost friend, tossing off his name quickly as though I must already know it, but too quickly to recognize. When he did this to several others, I realized he was the college president. In the first sweep of my assembled classmates not a familiar face emerged. Relieved, I stepped away and studied the campus architecture. Very little had changed but it was all oddly remote.

"Hi there."

A small, round woman about my age but with a remarkably smooth face and clear happy eyes was looking up at me.

"Hi, Gerry."

We quickly exchanged facts. She had married her high school boyfriend. They had four children, two in medical school. Girls. I offered a corresponding account. Her husband appeared and introduced himself. They were holding hands. He referred to her as Geraldine. We agreed it was the kind of day you can expect to end with a thunderstorm.

I discovered during this brief exchange that I was searching for something I wouldn't find talking with Gerry and her husband. I excused myself and walked away, deciding to skip lunch and look around.

I STROLLED through the library but it had been expanded so many times I found nothing familiar at all. Next I dropped in on a few of my favorite classrooms, pausing for a while in the Shakespeare room. The same vague photographs of English countryside and the faded blackboard made me think for a moment that our animated arguments about the nature of literature were still audible. Then I wandered out to the football practice fields. They were so unchanged that even the grass smelled the same. The stadium, too, looked just as it had though now empty except for the swallows picking feathery insects out of the windless June air.

Tentatively, I took my usual spot on the home team bench. For a strange moment I found I was looking back and forth at myself from either end of the forty years that had passed since I had last sat here.

What would the boy I was make of the person he had become?

At first he would seem disappointed.

"So you never played pro ball?"

"Nope. I know the coaches encourage you but, frankly, you're not that good."

"You could have been a coach."

"I know. Maybe it was a mistake but I chose not to. In fact, other things came up and it ceased being a choice at all."

Then I think he would have said, with some surprise and maybe a little disappointment: "So you're just a teacher. A professor. You teach in a great university?"

"It's not great but it's OK."

"What about Gerry?"

"Each of us married someone else."

"Someone else? How can that be? I've never met anyone like Gerry."

"I fell in love with another woman."

"What happened to Gerry? Wasn't she upset? I mean, gosh, she really loves me."

"She was upset. She sent back everything you ever gave her in a big box. The first thing, right on top, was your Milwaukee Braves cap."

"She . . . ?"

"But I doubt if she was very upset. She married that guy she was dating when you met her."

"The one from her hometown that goes to Harvard?"

"That one."

"She's much too good for him."

"She seems happy. She has four kids, all older than you."

"What's she like? Your wife, I mean."

"You're in for a surprise. She was like no one you ever thought of marrying. You have some growing up to do before you and this woman can love each other."

"You talk about her in the past tense."

"She's dead."

"She died?"

"Yes."

He sat quietly for a while. He was studying my face for something. I wondered what he saw there. I couldn't tell. I only knew his story of love had no place in it for this. Then when I told him about my children, so different from the children he and Gerry want to have, he seemed stunned by how much his life would change.

"Those dreams of yours," I said. "They're not such great dreams. But, then, not one will come true anyway. You may not want to have the life I have but I definitely prefer this to the life you dream of."

He turned toward me and smiled.

"You seem to have forgotten who I am," he said. "It's my dreams, such as they are, that led you to the dreams you live by now."

This was a surprise. I guess I expected to find a boy I wanted once more to be. I thought he still lived by the simpler dreams of his childhood, being a hero like Don Hutson. The boy I found already knew there is a deeper story that overrides all our dreams.

He knew there was a deeper story without knowing what the story was. It can be no other way. The lover's journey to the Beloved is circuitous, unpredictable, confusing. There are no maps. The lover can only advance by first being lost. There is no hero in this tale, only a fool.

"Don Hutson?"

"Don't you remember?"

YOU DIDN'T GO to see the Chicago Bears play the Green Bay Packers when Don Hutson was the Packers' star, you went to see Don Hutson play in the game between the Bears and the Packers. The final score mattered much less to the fans than the brilliant catches they expected Don to make.

They were rarely disappointed. He is arguably the greatest end ever to play the game.

I saw Don every chance I got. I had a lot of chances because he was a hero for the whole family and we bought our tickets early.

I cut a full-page picture of Don from the program of one of the games and glued it to the wall above my bed. It showed Don leaping skyward and looking back over his shoulder for the ball. His left knee was raised against his chest and his right toe was pointed straight back at earth. With his hands he had formed the perfect basket that every player emulated: the left arm extended full out and the right slightly under it and bent in the classical cradle shape. There wasn't the least doubt he would sweep the ball out of the air, complete the arc of this skyward leap, and head for glory.

I was fourteen when Don retired from professional football. We learned of it from a headline in our local newspaper. Editorials were full of phrases like "the close of an age" and "the last of the greats."

Not two months later a much larger headline dominated the front page of the same paper: HUTSON BUYS CADILLAC AGENCY IN CITY. We had not seen print this large since VJ Day. Editorials spoke of "the beginning of an era" and "the presence of greatness."

One hot summer day, my brother and I were out tossing a football to each other across our lawn and onto the lawn of the vacant house next door. The two yards together made an acceptably large touch football field. Hot as it was, we were adding further refinements to the Don Hutson catch.

We stopped to watch as a moving truck pulled up next door. The house had been empty for months and we were wild with curiosity to see if anyone our age was moving in. By the time most of the contents of the truck had been spread out on the lawn, it was obvious there was no adolescent in this household.

A yellow Cadillac convertible turned the corner at the end of the block and came slowly in our direction. It pulled in behind the moving truck and stopped softly at the curb. The top was down. A handsome man with a deep tan and sun-bleached hair sat behind the wheel. He opened the door, got out, and walked around the front of the car.

It was God.

My brother and I were standing at the edge of his yard, unable to breathe, motionless as the pieces of furniture all around us.

"Hi, boys."

That's all he said: "Hi, boys." In fact, in all the time the Hutsons lived next door to us, he never said anything but "Hi, boys." This was, of course, no ordinary "Hi." It was said in the slow, rich drawl of Don's native Alabama, and to the ear of a Wisconsin boy it could not have been more magnetizing or more exotic if he had been speaking Aztec.

Starting the next day, our yard became the site of an endless touch football game. Boys we hardly knew would stop us on the street to tell us their best dirty joke and split a Baby Ruth bar with us, on the outside chance we would include them in a game. Sometimes whole mornings, whole afternoons, ten or twenty of us would do nothing but practice our

Don Hutson catches between his house and ours. I could do killer imitations of Don opening the garage door, Don sliding into his Cadillac, Don touching his forehead and saying "Hi, boys."

That fall I went out for high school football for the first time. I marked off the days until the first practice. An unusually large number of boys appeared for tryouts so the equipment manager had to go back deeper into the storage rooms to suit up all of us. Instead of a uniform as such, you got a heap of parts, dozens of parts, in a big laundry bag. There were pads, straps, guards, shirts with numbers, shirts without numbers, things made of loosely attached pieces that had no apparent inside or outside, miscellaneous elastic bands and wraps, odd leather pieces that seemed to go nowhere. It was hard to think of Don putting on this stuff. Carefully but not too conspicuously watching others, I did manage to get most of it on. I had the most trouble with the helmet. It was a hinged sort of affair. If I put it on one way, it didn't protect my ears. The other way, I couldn't see. Finally, I found if I tightened the strap across the front of my chin I could make it serve both functions pretty well.

The coach told us to line up at our positions. Easily three-fourths of the boys were there to play end. When his lecture recommending other spots on the team didn't work, the coach said he would have last year's star quarterback throw all of us ends some passes so he could get a sense of our talent for the position.

This was my moment. I felt the thrilling whisper of destiny. When my turn came, I shot off downfield, pumping my knees. I turned sharply to the right, sprang perfectly from the earth, made the classic basket, and turned back just in time to see the ball sail beyond me. Crashing to the ground, I found myself rudely stuck, pinched, and jabbed by assorted pieces of uniform. Plenty of pain but no injury so I bounced up and raced back to the line.

On my second try, I got off the ground much more effectively, but a shoulder pad had come loose and popped up, blocking my vision, so I never saw the ball. The third time, I snagged a cleat on some kind of a pad that had slipped down around my ankle and took an unexpected roll three steps from the line. I was still not discouraged, however, since there was no question that, once I got this uniform business straightened out, my innate talent for the position would be obvious.

The coach lined us up and started assigning positions, pointing recklessly from boy to boy. "You. You play tackle," he said to someone in my direction. "No, you," he said. I thought for a moment he was talking to me. I looked around.

"That's right. You. The one with the helmet on backwards."

"IS THAT the way you remember it?" I asked the boy.

"Exactly what happened."

"And so you became a tackle, the player no one notices, always on the bottom of the pile."

I was a little surprised at the way I said this. Maybe I still thought he could do better. But the boy was smiling again.

"You don't look much like you could play tackle now," he said. "But I'll bet there's one thing that's never changed. I'll bet you still can't get your helmet on straight."

I wanted to argue with him, for there were instances when I knew I had it on right, when I truly knew what I was doing and did it. But there is something more important than getting it right: not knowing exactly what getting it right is. Somewhere, somehow, we always have our helmet on backwards—without knowing it. We are always wrong in some essential way about what our story is. We are never living out exactly the story we think we are. We are never exactly the character in that story we mean to be. But to be wrong in these ways is what makes it a story, openended and unpredictable, instead of a fixed plot rolling out to its foreknown conclusion. We don't know the path back to the Beloved; indeed, not knowing *is* that path. Knowing that we don't know is not only a higher ignorance, it is the basis for all our hope. This is what I really wanted to tell the boy.

"Like now," he said.

"Like now what?"

"You think you're just about to get all these thoughts straightened out at last but all you're really doing is sitting here in this thunderstorm."

THE CARHOP was fidgeting at the window. I had given her my order and was still trying to coax one out of Gerry. She leaned down and looked across the front seat, reciting the list of ice cream flavors to Gerry one more time.

"How about a weenie and a pop, honey?" I asked.

Gerry had pulled my Milwaukee Braves cap down over her ears and was moaning with indecision.

Finally, she raised her face enough that I could just see her eyes under the brim of the cap, and said, "Surprise me."

I never did surprise Gerry, but life did nothing but surprise both of us.

Shadows in the Eye of God

It is related that David was in the sanctuary. An ant passed in front of him. He lifted his hand with the intention of throwing the ant away from the place of prostation.

"O David," the ant protested, "what wantonness is this that you intend to inflict upon me? It is scarcely your task to lay hands upon me in God's own house!"

David was grief-stricken and said: "O God, how should I deal with Your creatures?" A voice was heard: "Make it your habit to act out of fear of God so that none has to suffer on your account! Do not locate the true source of creatures in their bodies! Look rather at the mystery of their creation! If We were to order an ant to come out of its black robe, so many indications of divine unity would radiate from its breast that the monotheists of the whole world would be put to shame."

SHARAFUDDIN MANERI

I walked down to the beaver pond with the boys to see what damage the thunderstorm had done during the night. Most of its heavy weaponry had been aimed at the mountain beyond but there was one terrifying hit somewhere around the pond. Except for the way everything was left washed and shining, a few fallen branches and leaves seemed to be all the storm had to show for itself.

"Dad, look. Great Blue's here."

The heron was standing with military formality on the far edge of the pond, its killer eye focused on something in our direction. We stepped softly to the edge of the pond. A branch cracked under my foot. The bird made a subtle move, as though annoyed, then spread those seven-foot wings and gave us a heartstopper takeoff, coming close enough we thought we could hear the whoosh of feather on air.

We watched as it lifted above the trees then the road and then the house and then up the mountain behind.

"Well, what do you make of that?" I asked.

"Make of what?"

"Have you seen Great Blue fly up that way before?"

"Yeah, he goes up there a lot."

"You sure?"

"Yeah."

"I'll be damned. Think about it. Why would he fly up the side of a mountain?"

"Because it's faster than walking?"

"No, I'm serious. That bird has nothing on his mind but lunch. And he doesn't eat squirrels, so figure it out."

They both looked at me dubiously as though there was a joke behind all this.

"He eats bears?"

"There's got to be a pond up there," I explained, "big enough to interest Great Blue and therefore big enough to have fish in it."

"But we've never seen one up there."

"We haven't seen the whole mountain."

I proposed they run up to the house and get their tackle. They bought the idea but not with enough conviction that they actually ran for their fishing gear. I grabbed a net, a hand shovel for worms, and a bucket for the fish (actually an old plastic diaper pail) and we headed out, while I wondered whether I had overstated my case. The plan was that we would follow a familiar logging road to the first vigorous brook then turn up the brook until we came to a pond or the brook ran out on us.

Within a few minutes we had passed out of the familiar circle of our woods and entered that part of the forest that looked like it had refused to belong to anyone. There had been some logging within the last fifty years or so but the misshapen ash, maples, and cherry, judged useless for lumber, clearly dated to the last century. These great eccentrics were obviously not finished with their defiance, standing there like jealous grandfathers over treeless circles of moss and fern. Patches of sun dropping accidentally out of a higher daylight gave the tunneled openings through these bigger trees an underwater feel. Now and then a jay swam across. Vireos whistled with mad repetitiveness in the canopy. Otherwise it was silent except for the few times a veery silvered the air with the descending spirals of its implausible song, runic secrets forgotten half a planet's age ago.

We had walked a half mile before we came to a brook worth a scramble upward. The brook was steep enough here to toss everything out of its own way but the hugest rocks, its water more heard than seen. What you could see were dark pools that stopped your eye for a moment and made you think trout. It was promising. So we started up, making a path of the rocks.

There is hypnosis in rocks. Stepping from one to another you reach your balance then lose it. Losing it, you aim yourself at the next foothold, careful to find one that won't roll away from you or send you slipping backwards. You commit yourself, pass through dimensionless space, light, reach your balance and lose it again. The very danger of it commits you to a lucid mindfulness in which you are nothing but foot or rock and it doesn't matter which. So we climbed, stopping only for breath and a surveying glance at the forest on either side, not thinking about what we were doing, not thinking at all.

That's why we didn't notice we were there until we had clawed up an earthen notch and were standing exposed to the all-knowing light trying to look at what we were seeing.

"Holy shit," Keene said, for all of us.

We were at the head of a beaver pond that reached back into the forest a hundred yards or more. The dam, bowing around on either side, had been built so long ago that all its woodsy substance had rotted into a wall so even it looked designed. A dense line of shrubs grew along it like a fence, a conspicuous opening here and there made by the beavers. The bottom of the pond, scrubbed by a century of winters, had become a medallion of golden sand now catching the full measure of the morning sun, open and clear as the eye of God.

"Dad. You sure this is it? I don't see Great Blue."

"This is it, Jamie. This is definitely it."

We had a brief strategy meeting. We would look for a blanket of damp leaves and go in for a handful of worms. Jamie would take one side of the pond and Keene the other. In minutes the boys had managed to thread onto their hooks three or four worms of the lively, dark red variety.

"Daddy, look." Jamie was holding up the squirming mass of worms, giving them an exaggerated hungry face look.

"Dad, how do you know there are any fish here?"

"I just know, that's all." The truth is, however, the water looked almost too bright so I had a small doubt of my own. Once the boys found spots where they could get sufficient space for a cast, I slowly scouted the edges.

Closer to the dam I noticed there were thick mats of vegetation that had grown out over the water. Very carefully, I inched out on one of them, worried it might break away and give me a headlong dunking. It was plenty solid. I hung over the edge and waited until my eyes adjusted to the darker shadows beneath me.

It could have been a full minute before I realized I was staring into the face of another being. I knew someone was looking at me before I knew what I was seeing. There was a space, an empty moment of who knows what duration, in which I existed only in the vision of another. I had to cross that space, incarnate that vision into the trout I was looking at, before I could look at all.

"Boys," I said in a stage-whispery monotone. They turned toward me and froze. "There's a trout here that's got to be eighteen inches or more, two feet. My God, there are several more. There could be dozens under here." I moved slightly and as suddenly as that there was only darkness, not a fish visible anywhere in it.

Both hooks came jerking back across the pond, got a new supply of worms, and the boys started casting in my direction. I told them I thought they didn't have to get that close and risk treeing their hooks. The trout can see the whole pond from where they are and if they want your bait all you have to do is have it in the water.

Keene took over a new piece of shore and cast his worm in a long smooth arc into the center of the pond, while Jamie worked his side with feverish industry. I watched from the dam, thinking that if one of these big guys hit I might have to help get it out of the water before it got hopelessly snagged up under a bank.

Now Jamie started casting into the middle and Keene began lazily trolling along the shore. I sat back against a tree and waited. Soon Keene was throwing dirt bombs down into the woods, accompanying them with an impressive repertoire of war noises. But his younger brother, sober and businesslike, had developed a smooth routine of casting, waiting, reeling, casting. I could tell I was in for a long morning.

AS I REMEMBER what happened next, I knew what I was seeing only after it was over. There wasn't much to it. A shadow passed over the sunlit bottom of the pond; the glob of worm disappeared; Jamie's line went slack then straight again, taut and vibrating.

"Jamie, you have a fish!" I started yelling. But Jamie had about as much reaction to what had happened as the trees behind him. He just stood there, both hands holding tight to the rod like someone was trying to take it from him. Not only did he say nothing, he didn't even seem to be breathing.

Both Keene and I were yelling at him now. "Reel it in! Don't let it run to the bank! Jamie! Quick! Pull back!" The line was doing wild Zs across the face of the water.

Too excited to do anything as complicated as slowly reel in the fish, Jamie resorted to a more elemental tactic. He turned away from the pond and, still gripping the rod with both hands, he rocketed down into the woods, crashing blindly through the undergrowth. The line must have caught in a tree somehow because I saw the fish leave the water vertically and twist upward into the sky, tossed by a recoiling branch. Then it seemed that pond and forest itself were in motion, turning under the trout as it swam its opposite element in an ecstasy of irresistance.

When I caught up to Jamie he was still bolting along full out as though he wanted to do the whole mountain in giant steps. We found the fish, still hooked, flopping weakly in a patch of fern. Jamie, sucking whole chestfuls of air, leaned against my shoulder as I brushed the leaves and grass off the trout. I was partly aware that Keene had begun a frantic activity of his own, flipping back rocks to find a worm "big as a snake."

"That's one hell of a catch, Jamie," I said holding up the trout by the gills. Jamie was still speechless, leaning over where he could stare down into the fish's sucking mouth.

"What is it, Daddy?"

"See this stripe here? That means it's a brook trout. And these red dots inside the line? That tells us it's a native brook trout."

"What's native?"

"Well, that's when the fish was born here and not raised somewhere else and brought here in a truck. Being native really means they have been here forever."

"Forever?"

"We've got a problem here, Jamie. It really swallowed your hook. You can sort of see where it is. Down there just below the gills." I pulled firmly against the hook and felt the reaction, like an electric current, in the fish's body.

"Does the fish hurt, Daddy?"

"I don't know if it hurts. It sure doesn't like this."

By getting two fingers deep into its throat and making a bold twist of it, I got the hook out.

"Do you think he'll live?"

"For a while, anyway. Go fill the bucket with water. That way we can keep him alive at least until lunch."

I found Keene working the pond with an energy that looked more like jealous rage than sport. Still, I let him have his chance. Besides, I knew there were more of these giants hiding in the dark corners of the pond. A dozen times or more he cast his worm into the most promising shadows before I could see his hope running down. He finally gave up when I promised he could help me clean the fish.

"Can we have him for lunch?"

"Sure," I said. "It's about time, too. It looks like it's already past twelve o'clock. You guys must be pretty hungry."

When I checked on Jamie, I found him kneeling over the bucket, his nose hardly an inch above the water. He was talking to the trout. I noticed a couple worms twisting at the bottom of the bucket.

"Are you feeding it, Jamie?"

"Yeah, but his mouth is too sore to eat."

"Does the fish have a name?"

"He's called Golden Shadow."

"Golden Shadow. That's a beautiful name, Jamie. Are you ready to go?"

"I guess so."

I suggested I carry the fish, promising I would be careful not to spill too much water. The boys quickly gathered their tackle, not bothering to break down their rods. We began our deliberate way down the brook to the wood road and then to the farm—Jamie, Keene, and I, and Golden Shadow.

I CAN'T REMEMBER when I first went fishing with my father. I can remember when I started cleaning fish. This stands out because it was the kind of ritual that makes a boy into a boy. First, there is the matter of the knife. It's always the best knife you have, sharpened so perfectly it can cut everything except itself. This is danger in its most elemental form. You can slice your flesh to the bone before you know it, especially if the fish is still alive when you start, usually the best time to clean a fish. So you learn quickly how to aim the knife and to cut away from yourself.

My preferred method was to start the cut just behind the head, severing the spine, then to come down behind the gills to the opening into the belly. If you have the right knife and know what you're doing, you can do it in one movement. You push the head to the side and while it makes a few last sucking motions, go in for the guts by way of a slice back to the anus.

Cleaning fish has an elegant brutality about it. The whole life of the fish adds up to nothing more than an unlovely handful of congealed slime. Like a fallen priest desacralizing the holy elements of someone else's religion, you can brush vast mysteries off your casual altar without a twinge of faith. Of course, there is always a threat you will freeze up on the question of origin: if this is how its life ends, how does it begin? But here the knife saves you. Its defining edge has no other concern than resistance to itself. So you follow it and live by its distinctions. Its distinctions are absolute; what it divides stays divided.

Cleaning fish was for me one of earliest lessons in learning how you become a man. It was the simplest of lessons. It began with the fact that I never liked cleaning fish. I hated it, in fact. The masculinity of the act for me had nothing to do with the act itself but with overriding my aversion to it. Before I could gut the fish I had to gut something in myself. That it was an aversion to killing made it an especially promising lesson. Before I can reduce the world, I must reduce myself. Or I get hurt.

I lifted the trout from the bucket and laid it out on the wooden block I used for cleaning. Before the first cut, I thought we should know for certain just how big this fish was. I had the fish tape in the same tackle box with the knife.

"Eighteen inches. Jamie, that is some catch. I can't remember that I have seen or heard of a trout this big caught anywhere around here. Nice going."

The boys' sister, Alisa, ran out from the house and stood just behind them looking cautiously over their shoulders like she was about to see something she might not want to see.

I set the trout up on its belly, got my best grip, thumb and forefinger in the soft part just behind the gills. I studied the blade of the knife. Excellent. As I set the knife against its favored spot, the fish kicked with enough force that it nearly leapt free of my hold. I felt an energy entering me with an intimacy so disturbing I had to suck back my own breath. For a terrifying moment I could not find the boundary between my life and the trout's. Then came the welcome surge of an ancient but familiar fury and I rode down into the either/or of it, stepping mercifully back into the primitive masculine joy of cutting away from myself the unwelcome wondering about where things begin and end. I took another grip on the fish, steeling my hand and arm, until I was sure it was just the two of us.

I pulled the fish back toward myself and away from the three pairs of skinny legs lined up at the edge of the cleaning block. Then I hesitated and checked the knife again. I don't know why I hesitated. Maybe I wasn't sure it would do all the cutting I needed.

"Dad?" Alisa said.

"What, honey?"

"Why couldn't you put it in the beaver pond?"

"I'm not really that hungry, Daddy," Jamie added with a pronounced eagerness.

I looked up at their faces. The fish kicked again. I dropped the knife to get a firmer grip. I could feel the gills opening and closing against my fingers.

"All right, bring the bucket."

Jamie led the way across the road and down to the pond, carrying the bucket with two hands. "Dad, will Great Blue eat him?"

"No, it's much too big for Great Blue."

Jamie walked to the edge of the pond then paused, contemplating just how he should do this. Then he waded out until he was up to his knees. He pushed the bucket down, carefully letting water spill in over the top, and tipped it out toward the center of the pond.

From where I was standing I could see Golden Shadow hanging pensively at the edge of the bucket. This was certainly not the clear water of his home. I wondered if he knew the difference. That was not all I wondered. Jamie reached slowly into the bucket to guide the fish out.

Jamie took a step back and the trout hung there for a second. A single flash of its tail sent it slowly outward. As it merged with the shadows in the deeper center of the pond, I could hear Jamie whispering, "You'll be all right now, Golden Shadow. You'll be all right now."

THAT NIGHT my wife and I as usual took our coffee out onto the open porch in front of the house. We sat in silence watching as the darkness brought the trees around the pond into profile. Charlie performed his evening ritual of appearing just before dark, sitting between us with his eyes alertly fixed on the shutters where the bats were making their little sounds of preparation. For a while we could hear the children's voices from the bedrooms upstairs. Slowly the pauses got longer then they too entered the larger circle of our quiet.

I stood, touched my wife briefly, started to explain what I needed to do then realized an explanation wasn't necessary. I walked down the lawn toward the pond.

"Honey," Alice said softly.

"Yes?"

"I love you."

There was still enough light around the pond to tell whether the fish had bellied up. I leaned against the old beaver stump and studied the surface of the water. Soon the night speakers began declaring their thousand knowledges. Then there was no light but starlight. The Corona Borealis was near its zenith, Venus was dominant in the south, Orion was riding the dark ridge of pines behind me.

Suddenly everything went still as though some coded message had made listeners of us all. I heard something moving on the opposite bank. But then I wasn't sure. I held my breath to hear better. A presence. Deer? Raccoon? The great horned owl? The creature tongues resumed and I strained harder at the silence behind them. Then I knew I would never know.

Sources

BREAKFAST AT THE VICTORY

Sources cited: Kenneth Cragg, *Wisdom of the Sufis*, New York: 1976, p. 8; Jean-Paul Sartre, *Being and Nothingness*, New York: 1956, p. lxii; Lao Tsu, *Tao Te Ching*, ch. 37; *The Portable Nietzsche*, New York: 1956, pp. 178f.; Chuang-Tsu, *Inner Chapters*, New York: 1974, p. 29 (italics added); Nagarjuna, MMK, XXV, 19–20, quoted in Loy, *Nonduality*, New Haven: 1988, p. 184; Kierkegaard, *Fear and Trembling*, Princeton: 1983, p. 16.

A PHILOSOPHER NEEDS A CAT

Sources cited: Reynald A. Nicholson, *The Mystics of Islam*, New York: 1975, p. 109 (retold); Descartes, *Meditations on First Philosophy*, tr., John Cottingham, Cambridge: 1986, p. 77; Opening verses of the Kena Upanishad, slightly altered, from *The Thirteen Principal Upanishads*, tr., Robert E. Hume, Oxford: 1985; *The Sufi Path of Love* (selections from the writings of Jalal al-Din Rumi), ed., William C. Chittick, Albany: 1983, p. 132; Lao Tsu, *Tao Te Ching*, ed., Stephen Mitchell, New York: 1988, chs. 1 (altered), 48, and 34; *The Cloud of Unknowing*, tr., Clifton Wolters, Middlesex: 1961, p. 60.

AN EYE FOR KILLING BUDDHAS

Sources cited: *The Upanishads*, tr., Juan Mascaro, Middlesex: 1965, p. 119; Sharafuddin Maneri, *The Hundred Letters*, op. cit., p. 62; Meister Eckhart, quoted in David Loy, op. cit., New Haven: 1988, p. 238; Abu Bakr al-Wasiti, quoted in Schimmel, *The Mystical Dimensions of Islam*, op. cit., p. 173; Shibli, quoted in Schimmel, p. 172; *Chuang-tsu: Inner Chapters*, tr., Gia-Fu Feng and Jane English, New York: 1974, p. 116; William Blake, *The Portable Blake*, ed., Alfred Kazin, New York: 1946, p. 135.

A HIGHER IGNORANCE

Sources cited: Robert K. C. Forman, ed., *The Problem of Pure Consciousness*, New York: 1990, p. 141; Sartre, *Being and Nothingness*, pp. lxii, 28 (slightly altered), 90; *Meister Eckhart*, tr., Raymond Blakney, New York: 1941, p. 107.

THE WAY THE SOUL SEES

Sources cited: Annemarie Schimmel, *Mystical Dimensions of Islam*, Chapel Hill: 1975, p. 49; Blaise Pascal, *Pensées*, tr., W. F. Trotter, New York: 1941, #205.

A DEEPER DREAMER

Source cited: A. L. Basham, *The Origins and Development of Classical Hinduism*, New York: 1989, p. 23 (selections).

VISION IN A DEATHWRAP

Sources cited: Herman Melville, *Moby Dick*, New York: 1926, pp. 157f.; Annemarie Schimmel, *The Mystical Dimensions of Islam*, op. cit., p. 112; Nicholas Cusa, *The Vision of God*, tr., Emma Gurney Salter, New York: 1960, pp. 16, 26 (slightly altered), 27; *Meister Eckhart*, Blakney, op. cit., p. 230; Plotinus, ed., O'Brien, p. 78.

HOW FAR WE ARE FROM GOD

Sources cited: Kenneth Cragg, *Wisdom of the Sufis*, New York: 1976, p. 48; Reynold A. Nicholson, *The Mystics of Islam*, London, 1975, p. 88.

LIKE A RANDOM BEAR

Sources cited: *Open Secret: Versions of Rumi*, tr., John Moyne and Coleman Barks, Putney: 1984, p. 10; Robert K. C. Forman, ed., *The Problem of Pure Consciousness*, New York: 1990, p. 115.

A SHARED SILENCE

Sources cited: Sharafuddin Maneri, *The Hundred Letters*, tr., Paul Jackson, New York: 1980, pp. 369f.

This book would not exist were it not for Robin Nagle's perceptive reading of the earliest drafts of the manuscript and her continuing encouragement. Her thoughtful attention to its language and voice has been indispensable. With remarkable patience, Carol Mack repeatedly challenged me to clarify and strengthen the book's ideas and narrative sequences. Major revisions resulted. Tom Driver, Mary Parker, and Jonathan Collett worked the manuscript over with their customary intellectual rigor and a fine eye for nonsequiturs. Many thanks to Nancy Gazells, Elaine Bomford, Maria Cheng, and Anna Roelofs for their generous and critical reading of parts of the manuscript. A special salute to my agent, Knox Burger, for shepherding this work through its final stages and to Amy Hertz and John Loudon for their skillful and professional editing.

The writing was greatly assisted by a grant from the Rockefeller Foundation for a residency at the Bellagio Study and Conference Center.

The identity of several persons has been altered just enough to protect them from public recognition but not enough that they would not recognize themselves.